First published 1923
Reprinted 1924, 1925, 1930
1935, 1947, 1949

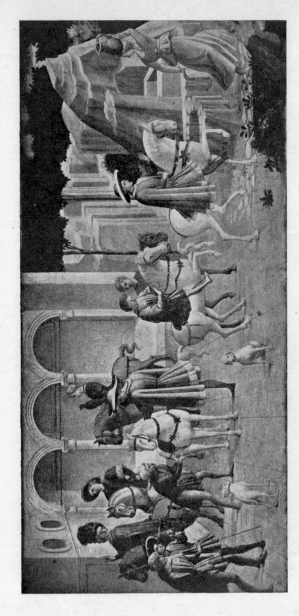

On the left: the Marquis prepares to go riding (ll. 267–73). On the right: he salutes Griselda (cp. ll. 274–90). From the painting by Pesellino at Bergamo.

CHAUCER

The Clerkes Tale

of Oxenford

EDITED BY

KENNETH SISAM

OXFORD

AT THE CLARENDON PRESS

CONTENTS

ILLUSTRATIONS

Printed in Great Britain at the OXFORD UNIVERSITY PRESS
By Charles Batey, Printer to the University

INTRODUCTION

'TO Bartholomew Fair, to walk up and down; and there, among other things, find my Lady Castlemaine at a puppet-play, *Patient Grizill*': so Mr. Pepys on 30th August, 1667, records the enduring popularity of the story of Griselda, and its trick of finding admirers in unlikely quarters. In Italy, its native home, the story has been a chap-book and a subject for the decoration of cottage walls down to the present day. Already before 1400 France knew it in a play called *Le Mystère de Grisildis*, and a prose version *Le Ménagier de Paris*. To Spanish literature it contributed the plot of Lope de Vega's *Pattern for Married Women* (1615). In German, Halm wove it into a background of Arthurian legend to make his play *Griselda* (1835), which is accounted a classic. Nor has England been behind the Continent in testimonies of admiration. Chaucer led the way with *The Clerkes Tale*, and probably inspired the school play on Griselda by his admirer John Radcliff, of which there is mention in the first half of the sixteenth century. The Stationers' Register for 1565-6 records a 'ballett intituled *The Sounge of Pacyente Gressell unto hyr Make*', which was followed by Thomas Deloney's ballad 'to the tune of *The Bride's Goodmorrow*'. *The Commodye of Pacient Grissill*[1] by John Phillip probably appeared in 1565-6. A much better play, the *Patient Grissill* of Dekker, Chettle and Haughton, was printed in 1603. A favourite prose version, found first in an edition dated 1619,[2] provided the text for a line

---

[1] Malone Society, 1909.   [2] Percy Society, 1842.

of chap-books that continued far into the eighteenth century. In 1794 a modernization of *The Clerkes Tale* was thought worthy of a place in *Angelica's Ladies' Library*. And there are many later reprints or adaptations.

It was Boccaccio (1313–75), Chaucer's one rival among mediaeval story-tellers, who gave the tale to European literature. Diligent investigators have tried to trace it farther back, and have adduced parallels more or less remote : the *Lai le Fresne*; the *Nut Brown Maid*; the *Ballad of Fair Annie*; even the Tale of Constance, which the Man of Law tells in *The Canterbury Tales*, though her patience was rather a pattern for shipwrecked mariners than for wives. Yet after all they are bound to admit that our story is first found in the *Decameron*. Not that it is new in kind : it belongs to the race of *exempla* —moral stories, of which hundreds were composed or adapted during the Middle Ages to illustrate the several vices and virtues. Griselda is patience personified, and might have shared oblivion with other personifications of the time, had not a great artist been her creator.

Boccaccio chose a sombre background for the gaiety of the *Decameron*.—Florence is in the grip of the Black Death of 1348. Seven young ladies of quality happen to meet in a church, and one proposes that, instead of helplessly awaiting the chance of infection, they should visit some of their country estates near by, to be free from the sights and sounds of death. Three young men join the party ; and, leaving the plague-stricken city behind, they spend a fortnight in sun-lit fields and shady gardens. Ten days are given to story-telling, and each day ten stories are told. On the last evening, when only one tale is wanting to complete the hundred, the youth Dioneo introduces

the story of Griselda with the easy brevity that marks
Boccaccio's prose:

> 'Gentle my ladies, this day, meseems, is dedicate to Kings
> and Soldans, and folk of the like quality; wherefore, that I stray
> not too far from you, I am minded to tell you somewhat of
> a Marquis; certès, nought magnificent, but a piece of mad folly,
> albeit there came good thereof to him in the end. The which
> I counsel none to copy, for that great pity 'twas that it turned
> out well with him.' [1]

We must not infer from Dioneo's words that Boccaccio
thought poorly of his creation. The last place, as
Petrarch remarked,[2] is the place of honour; and it was
consummate art that led him to set at the end of the
Decameron (which even in its own age was criticized
for its offences against good manners) a story that
may weary us by its unreality, yet cannot fail to leave
the impression of purity and repose.

In 1350, while he was at work on the *Decameron*,
Boccaccio met Petrarch, and a lifelong friendship
began. Petrarch was then the acknowledged chief
among European men of letters, and the leader of the
classical revival. But the first effect of the new
learning was to freeze up, rather than to open, the
sources of original production. Petrarch's judgement,
so sane in most things, was warped by his enthusiasm
for the Latin classics. He thought more of his own
Africa, an epic long since dead, than of the sonnets to
Laura and the letters to his friends on which his fame
now rests. He rescued Boccaccio from idleness, only
to press upon him such dreary tasks as the *De Casibus*

---

[1] Rigg's translation.

[2] 'It always pleased me when I heard it years ago, and I should
think it pleased you too, since you deemed it worthy of your Italian
prose, and of the end of your book, where the teaching of the rhetoricians
requires that matter of greater import should be placed.' *Epistolae
Seniles* xvii. 3 (to Boccaccio).

*Petrarch, laurel-crowned, visits Boccaccio, and rouses him from
idleness, whose charms are represented by the female figure in the
doorway inscribed ' Peresse ', modern Fr. ' paresse '*

From the Munich Boccaccio.

Boccaccio, roused by Petrarch, goes on composing his 'De Casibus Virorum Illustrium'. In the background the characters of his stories come thronging in.

From the Munich Boccaccio.

Virorum Illustrium, which (as the picture at p. xii shows faithfully) was addressed to an audience very different from the gay company that first heard the *Decameron*. So the most brilliant prose writer of the age, who had from nature the speed and lightness that learning cannot give, spent his later years compiling a book of classical mythology (*De Genealogiis Deorum*) and a dictionary of classical topography.

Petrarch's coldness towards works in the vernacular is scarcely disguised in the opening of the letter to Boccaccio [1] that contains his Latin prose version of the Griselda story. It was written in 1373, when the *Decameron* had been published for twenty years:

> 'A copy of the book which you published—in your younger days I think it was—has somehow or other come under my eye. It would be untrue to say I have read it: for it is a big book, and written in the popular style; besides I have been very busy, and the times oppress me. . . . I ran over it like a traveller in a hurry, glancing here and there, and nowhere tarrying long. And, as commonly happens when one skims a book, I looked at the beginning and end rather more closely than the rest.'

At the beginning he praises the description of Florence under the Plague ; at the end the story of Griselda :

> ' It so pleased me and held my attention that among all my cares, which sometimes make me almost forget myself, I decided to commit it to memory, that I might repeat it for my own pleasure whenever I liked, and, on occasion, tell it to my friends.'

His friends too were delighted with it ; and soon he conceived the idea of making a Latin prose version 'that so sweet a story may give pleasure to those who know no Italian '. This version, which he called ' A Fable of Wifely Obedience and Fidelity ' (*de Obedientia ac Fide uxoria Mythologia*), he sends to Boccaccio.

---

[1] *Epistolae Seniles* xvii. 3.

His expectation of reaching a wider public was justified in the result. Latin was then the common language of European literature ; and although Petrarch's version is inferior to its original, missing the terse vigour of Boccaccio's prose, in making the story known outside Italy it played the greater part.

To Petrarch the Clerk makes acknowledgement in his prologue:

> I wol yow telle a talĕ which that I
> Lerned at Padwe of a worthy clerk . . .
> Fraunceys Petrak, the lauriat poéte;

and again near the end of his tale:

> . . . therfore Petrak writeth
> This storie, which with heigh stile he enditeth.

And the briefest comparison of the texts confirms his words. There is ample proof that Chaucer knew some of Boccaccio's works: his *Teseide* is the source of *The Knight's Tale*; his *Filostrato* is the main source and the *Filocolo* a secondary source of *Troilus*; his Latin works *De Casibus Virorum Illustrium* and *De Claris Mulieribus* are both drawn upon for *The Monk's Tale*. But Chaucer knew nothing of their author,[1] and appears to have read no part of the *Decameron*. To many critics such ignorance seems incredible. But with the letter just cited before us, in which Boccaccio's closest friend avows his own slight acquaintance with the *Decameron*, and implies that to other Italians of literary taste the Griselda story was a novelty, we cannot be surprised that Chaucer in distant England was so ill informed. Before the days of printing, books were published in

---

[1] In *Troilus* v. 1653 he quotes a mysterious 'Lollius' as his authority, when he is in fact following Boccaccio's *Filostrato*. In *Troilus* i. 394 he attributes Petrarch's 88th Sonnet to the same Lollius. In *The Monk's Tale* 335 he makes Petrarch the author of Boccaccio's *De Casibus*.

comparatively few copies. Their dissemination was irregular ; so that Chaucer's access to a volume containing the *Filocolo*, *Filostrato*, and *Teseide* affords no ground to assume that the *Decameron* was also acces-

Boccaccio relating the misfortunes of the great. Scenes from the narrative in the background.

From a fifteenth-century miniature in Brit. Mus. MS. Add. 35321.

sible to him. Contemporary judgements of value differed from ours, and many channels open to such a book as the *De Casibus* [1] would be closed to the

---

[1] The *De Casibus* exists in many beautiful MSS., of which two are represented in the pictures at pp. viii, ix, xii, 78. I cannot recall any copy of the *Decameron* in England earlier than that which Duke Humphrey of Gloucester (†1447) had from his 'very dear cousin the Earl of Warwick'. It is now at Paris, Bibl. Nat. MS. français 12,421.

Decameron. Besides there was little curiosity about what we call literary history—the lives of authors, the facts of authorship.

This last point bears on the question whether or not Chaucer met Petrarch. Petrarch made his version in the spring of 1373; from 1st December 1372 to 23rd May 1373 Chaucer was absent from England on a mission to Genoa: and it would be pleasing to think that he visited Petrarch at Padua, and learned the tale from him. If it be urged that *The Clerkes Tale* is shown by internal evidence to be a translation from a manuscript, and not from memory, the answer is that Petrarch may have given Chaucer an advance copy. If this hypothesis must be abandoned because Chaucer used a corrupt manuscript,[1] then he may have heard the tale from Petrarch, and obtained a copy at some later date. It has been objected that he had business enough to fill so short a time, without making an excursion to Padua, for in those days the journey was a long one. No doubt its difficulties would have been overcome by a modern hunter after literary celebrities: but is it not an anachronism to attribute the same desires and zeal to Chaucer? Petrarch's *Letters* are well preserved, yet they give no hint that Chaucer was even one of his correspondents. And there is something peculiarly modern in the idea that a government envoy would make the arduous journey from Genoa to Padua in order to exchange greetings with a distinguished literary man to whom he was a stranger.[2]

---

[1] See the note to l. 1148.

[2] Had the personal communication of the Griselda story really taken place, it seems unlikely that Petrarch, who tells Boccaccio how it affected a Paduan friend and another from Verona (note to l. 1142), would omit to record its effect on the English visitor who had made a literary pilgrimage so flattering to his vanity.

Of course there are some who hold that the Clerk's words and experiences (though they suit his own character admirably)[1] must, in this interesting point, be the words and experiences of Chaucer; but their method of making literary history is least happy when applied to a great poet, who may at any time upset it by inventing for his characters experiences not his own. Much simpler, and as likely to hit the truth, is Landor's way in his *Imaginary Conversations* (the Second Series), where, without justificative pieces, he makes Petrarch, Chaucer, and Boccaccio meet and exchange stories at Arezzo.

To belief in the meeting with Petrarch in 1373 is ultimately due the assignment of *The Clerkes Tale* to a date soon after that year. From the body of the tale the supporters of this early date distinguish the prologue, which refers to Linian's death in 1383; the two stanzas on the fickleness of the people, which would apply most naturally to the troubled reign of Richard II; the two stanzas at the end, containing a reference to the Wife of Bath; and the Envoy: and they assume that these passages were added to the earlier draft when Chaucer worked it into the plan of *The Canterbury Tales*, perhaps about 1387. The exclusion of all the passages bearing any mark of time may seem a drastic way of upholding the hypothesis of early date; but it is reasonable enough to be worth weighing against the alternative hypothesis that these passages (or some of them) were added as Chaucer made his translation; in other words, that *The Clerkes Tale* was written after the plan of *The Canterbury Tales* had taken shape.

If the meeting with Petrarch in 1373 be rejected as pure fancy, and I think it must be, then the

---

[1] See note to l. 27.

arguments for an early date seem to be these :—First, that the translation is literal, by comparison, for instance, with the freedom of *Troilus*: to which it may be answered that *The Knight's Tale*, generally held to be early, is freely translated ; and that after two masters had handled the Griselda story, Chaucer found it in good shape and of convenient length. Secondly, that the stanza form is a mark of early date. How little weight the exponents of this view attach to it is shown by their assignment of *The Prioress's Tale*, in the identical stanza, to a comparatively late date. After all Chaucer was a good enough craftsman to realize the advantages of metrical variety, and to realize also that the rather tenuous story of Griselda would gain by being told in a metre more elaborate than the rimed couplet. Thirdly, there is the argument that the tale is not Chaucer's best work, and is not very characteristic of what is assumed to be his latest style. This is a matter of opinion ; but at least we must remember that he would have ruined the story of Griselda by overloading it with his characteristic humour ; and that for those authors whose compositions can be exactly dated, highest quality and latest date do not always run together.

On the other side must be set the perfect appropriateness of the matter to the character of the Clerk ; the neatness with which it fits into the general plan of the Tales; the evidence of all the passages in which marks of time could appear; and one piece of external evidence. *The Legend of Good Women* can hardly be earlier than 1386. In its prologue Chaucer pretends that the God of Love rated him for speaking ill of lovers—and particularly of women—in his translation of *The Romaunt of the Rose* and in *Troilus*. Alceste (who stands for the Queen) decides that he must write a *Legend of Good Women* to put his fairness beyond doubt; but first she defends him by citing the works he has already produced:

> He made the book that hight the Hous of Fame,
> And eek the Deeth of Blaunchè the Duchesse,
> And the Parlèment of Foules, as I gesse,
> And al the Love of Palamoun and Arcite
> Of Thebes, thogh the storye ys knowen lyte;
> And many an ympnè for your halidayes,
> That highten balades, roundels, virelayes;
> And for to speke of other holynesse,
> He hath in prosè translated Boece,
> And made the Lyfe also of Seynt Cecile.
> He made also, goon ys a gretè while,
> Origenes upon the Maudeleyne.
> Hym oughtè now to have the lessè peyne.

This is not mere argument. It is a way of bringing to the notice of the court the extent and merit of his literary work; and the absence of any mention of the Griselda story, which from its subject-matter would have a special relevance, is good evidence that it was not published in 1386. It may, of course, have been written earlier and kept in store; but the onus of proof is on those who contend for an earlier date than 1386.

By 1386 the plan of *The Canterbury Tales* had probably taken shape. It is set out by the Host towards the end of the *Prologue*, after the company of pilgrims assembled at the Tabard Inn, in Southwark, had agreed to accept his happy idea for their entertainment on the way to and from Canterbury:

> Ech of yow, to shortè with oure weye,
> In this viàge shal tellè tales tweye,—
> To Caunterbury-ward, I mene it so,
> And homward he shal tellen othere two,—
> Of áventùres that whilom han bifalle:
> And which of yow that bereth hym best of alle,
> That is to seyn, that telleth in this caas
> Tales of best senténce and moost soláas,
> Shal have a soper at oure aller cost,
> Heere in this placè, sittynge by this post,
> Whan that we come agayn fro Caunterbury.

There were 'wel nine and twenty' in the company
—thirty on a stricter count—and of most of them
the *Prologue* gives full-length portraits. Besides there
was Chaucer, who was to be their chronicler: now
nearly fifty, a short man, and running to flesh; hold-

Chaucer on Pilgrimage. From the Ellesmere MS.

ing a little aloof from the rest the better to observe
them; yet with eyes seemingly riveted to the ground,[1]
and a way of laughing at himself which must have put
his companions at their ease. Thus altogether the

---

[1] See for all this the Host's remarks when he calls on Chaucer to tell
his first tale, *Sir Thopas*.

pilgrims should have told at least a hundred and twenty tales; but the plan was contracted to cover the outward journey only; and to one tale apiece[1]; and even in its less ambitious form it was never completed. Only twenty-one tales were finished, and one of these is the Canon's Yeoman's, who, with his master, first joined the company at Boughton-under-Blean. Three more were left unfinished—the Cook's, the Squire's, and *Sir Thopas*.

The Pilgrims' Way to Canterbury.

Some of the tales are linked together by direct allusions (like the Merchant's references to *The Clerkes Tale* in his prologue), or by conversations in which the Host usually takes the lead; but there are gaps between the groups, and it is not known exactly how Chaucer proposed to arrange them. Modern editions refer to an order which is derived from the notes of time and place that appear in the text. Although our pilgrims were all well enough off to hire horses at Southwark, the road was so bad that four days would be a fair time to allow for the journey to Canterbury.

[1] Only Chaucer tells two tales, *Sir Thopas* and *Melibeus*; but the first was interrupted. When he calls on the Parson, a little way off Canterbury, the Host says 'every man save thou hath toold his tale'.

And if we accept Dr. Furnivall's arrangement, the tales were told as follows:

Day i. **A.** Tales of the Knight, Miller, Reeve, Cook ...
Halt for the night at Dartford.

ii. **B.** Tales of the Man of Law, Shipman, Prioress, Chaucer (two), Monk, Nun's Priest. *Halt for the night at Rochester.*

iii. **C.** ? Tales of the Doctor and Pardoner?; **D.** Wife of Bath, Friar, Sumner; **E.** Clerk, and Merchant. *Halt for the night at Ospringe.*

iv. **F.** Tales of the Squire ... Franklin ; **G.** Second Nun, Canon's Yeoman; **H.** Manciple ; and **I.** Parson. *Arrival at Canterbury.*

So it is near Sittingbourne, perhaps in the stretch of

Ferris photo

The well of St. Thomas beside the Pilgrims' road, Bapchild.

road that runs through Bapchild and by the old Well of St. Thomas, that we may imagine the Clerk telling his tale.

And now we can see how skilfully Chaucer worked *The Clerkes Tale* into its setting. The Wife of Bath had begun the third day with her prologue proclaiming the domination of wives over their husbands; she had denounced clerks generally for their railing at women, and in particular had told how she gained the mastery over 'a clerk of Oxenford' (her fifth husband), and made him burn his 'cursed book' of stories against her sex. The Friar comments courteously enough on the length of her preamble; whereupon the Sumner, his rival by profession, flares up: 'a flye and eek a frere Wol falle in every dyssh and eek matéere'. The Friar threatens to tell a tale or two about a sumner; the Sumner retorts that he will tell two or three tales about friars before he gets to Sittingbourne; and the Host has to intervene: 'Lat the womman telle hire tale.' As soon as her tale is done, the Friar breaks in with his story of a sumner whom the Devil carried off for his sins; and the Sumner replies in kind. Perhaps lunch at Sittingbourne broke off the quarrel; but when they took the road again, the Host, who was a good master of ceremonies, must have felt that tempers were rising, and that the stories of the morning had not been very edifying. So, to redress the balance, he calls on the modest Clerk.[1]

The Clerk rises to the occasion. He tells a simple story that all of them can understand. By its quietness and old-fashioned ideals of goodness it contrasts perfectly with the tales of the morning. Yet the thread of sequence is maintained: it is the starting-point for the Merchant, who has been married but two months and has found his wife no Griselda; and, by another device of contrast, this 'Fable of Wifely Obedience and Fidelity', told by a clerk on the authority of 'a worthy clerk', makes the counterpoise

[1] It can hardly be early in the day, in view of the Host's remark: 'This day ne herd I of your tonge a word' 4; and it probably follows immediately after the bait for lunch at Sittingbourne.

to the Wife of Bath's *Prologue*. That Chaucer so
intended it is clear enough from the reference to the
Wife of Bath near the end, before the uproarious
Envoy begins; and a very discerning critic[1] has
argued that the Envoy itself is in perfect dramatic
keeping with the Clerk's character and purpose. Yet
perhaps the MSS. are right when they call it ' L'envoy
de Chaucer '. He could seldom resist the temptation
to intrude himself in order to give 'the other side';
and this metrical *tour de force* seems to be the
expression in concentrated form of all the criticisms
that regard for good story-telling had pent up.

But on these matters of opinion I leave the text to
speak: with a word of warning.—Chaucer, like all
great story-tellers, is easy to read rapidly. But when
closely examined he is a difficult writer, sometimes
extraordinarily subtle where he seems to be casual, at
other times saying things apparently 'ful of hy sentence'
just because some reason of technique made it convenient to say them. In this tale, for instance, he
follows Petrarch very closely. But if we note the
places where he adds matter of less than a stanza in
bulk, we shall find that they fall almost invariably at
the stanza's end.[2] The reason is simple: at the end
of the stanza the rime-scheme becomes more exacting,
and he found the original harder to manipulate than
matter of his own choosing. No verbal study of
Chaucer can succeed that does not take account of such
'considerations of the workshop '.

[1] Professor Kittredge, *Chaucer and his Poetry* (1915), pp. 193 ff.
[2] e.g. ll. 103, 147, 174–5, 215–17, 264–6, 290–4, 433–5, 460–2, 581,
622–3, 811–12, 852–4, 888–9, 916–17.

GEOFFREY CHAUCER, son of John Chaucer, wine merchant, of London, was born about 1340. By 1357 he had begun his career as a page in the household of Lionel, Duke of Clarence. In 1359 he was with the army in France: he was taken prisoner, and his ransom was paid in March 1360. In 1367 he received a pension as a member (*dilectus valettus*) of the King's household. In 1369, on the death of Blanche, wife of John of Gaunt, he wrote his *Deth of Blanche the Duchesse*, the first evidence of an important friendship with John of Gaunt.

He became a trusted member of the diplomatic service, visiting France several times (1369–78), Flanders (1377), Italy (1372–3 and 1378); and he was successful, if we may judge from the favours that came his way:—another pension, a pitcher of wine daily, the Comptrollership of the Customs of Wools, Skins, and Hides (1374); the wardship of two minors (1375); the proceeds of a heavy fine (1376); the sinecure Comptrollership of Petty Customs at London (1382); and the right to discharge his other more onerous Comptrollership by deputy (1385). In 1386 he became member of Parliament for Kent. During this prosperous period he wrote his version of *Boethius*; the *Hous of Fame*; the *Parlement of Foules*; *Troilus* (1385); and the *Legend of Good Women* (1386); and he probably planned the *Canterbury Tales*, his last great work.

But with the failure of John of Gaunt's party in the autumn of 1386, he lost both his Comptrollerships: and he saw lean days till 1389, when Richard II made him Commissioner of Works. This post, too, he lost in 1391: but in 1394 another pension was granted him. In his latter years he was often in debt. We need not picture him in misery, for debt is sometimes the result of living well. In 1399 he greeted the new king Henry IV with his last work, the *Compleynt to his Purse*. It gained him another pension, which he did not long enjoy. He died in 1400, and was buried in Westminster Abbey.

He had married Philippa, a lady of the court, perhaps in 1366. She died in 1387. For a 'litel son Lowis', then ten years old, he wrote the *Treatise on the Astrolabe* in 1391. Thomas Chaucer, Speaker of the House of Commons, 1407, &c., was his son.

SELECT BIBLIOGRAPHY[1]

BIBLIOGRAPHICAL.

Hammond, Miss E. P., *Chaucer: A Bibliographical Manual*, New York, 1908.

Wells, J. E., *A Manual of the Writings in Middle English, 1050-1400*, New Haven, &c., 1916; Supplements, 1919, &c.

Brusendorff, A., *The Chaucer Tradition*, London, 1925.

COMPLETE EDITIONS (in one volume).

Skeat, W. W., *The Student's Chaucer*, [Oxford Poets] Oxford, 1895.

Robinson, F. N., The Complete Works, &c., Cambridge (U.S.A.) and London, 1933.

STUDIES OF THE PERIOD.

Hutton, E., *Giovanni Boccaccio*, London, 1910.

Jusserand, J. J., *English Wayfaring Life in the Middle Ages* (transl. L. Toulmin Smith), London, 1889, &c.; revised edn. 1921.

Ker, W. P., *English Literature, Medieval*, London, 1912.

Trevelyan, G. M., *England in the Age of Wycliffe*, London, 1899; new edn. 1909.

CRITICAL STUDIES OF CHAUCER'S LIFE AND WORKS.

Dryden, John, Preface to his *Fables*, 1700.

Kittredge, G. L., *Chaucer and his Poetry*, Cambridge (U.S.A.) and London, 1915.

Legouis, E., *Chaucer* (transl. L. Lailavoix), London, 1913.

Lowell, J. R., Essay on *Chaucer* in *My Study Windows*, 1871 [Scott Library].

Lowes, J. L., *Geoffrey Chaucer*, London, 1934.

[1] In this list only books suitable for general reading are included. The bibliographical manuals cited give a full account of the great body of Chaucer criticism contained in special editions, monographs, and journals. As I have found it impossible to give specific references to these sources of information, I take this opportunity of making a general acknowledgement.

THE TEXT

SIXTEEN MSS. of *The Clerkes Tale* have been printed by the Chaucer Society, and the Latin source is followed so closely that their readings can be controlled better than in any other of the Tales. By reference to four typical MSS —Ellesmere, Hengwrt, Harley 7334, and Corpus (Oxford)—the principles on which the present text is established may be stated summarily. They do not necessarily apply to the other Tales, and they are put forward merely as an attempt to bring a question, usually left vague, into some order and definition.

(i) Ellesmere is made the basis, less for the merit of its peculiar readings than for its high average of correctness in spelling, grammar, metre, and arrangement ; and for the ease with which its readings can be checked by the nearly related Hengwrt MS.

(ii) The readings peculiar to Ellesmere are generally to be rejected either as scribal slips (e. g. omission of *suffre us* 36) ; or as intelligent misreadings (e. g. *consentynge* for *conformynge* 546 n.) ; or as variations, not bad in themselves, but not superior to better authenticated readings, e. g. *tale* for *mater* 341. The consensus of Hengwrt, Harley 7334, and Corpus in a satisfactory reading is decisive against Ellesmere, I think, even in ll. 552 f.

(iii) Ellesmere, Hengwrt, and Harley 7334 agree in some readings which are certainly bad (e. g. *humblenesse* 429 n. ; *and she moore of age* 916 n.). Hence behind these MSS. there lies, in some way, at least one recension by a hand other than Chaucer's.

(iv) Corpus has good readings in these places. Careless and defective as it is, it provides the means of getting behind this non-Chaucerian recension ; and the common belief that it is 'almost worthless' is not supported by the text of *The Clerkes Tale*.

(v) The famous Harley 7334, which has been thought to represent a revision by Chaucer, has several bad readings, and contributes nothing of value to our text.

(vi) The MSS. printed afford no evidence that *The Clerkes Tale* was circulated as a separate work before it was incorporated in the frame-work of the *Canterbury Tales*.

The Text

(vii) Chaucer's text is, in essentials, well preserved, and it is nowhere necessary to go outside the printed MSS. in order to find a satisfactory reading.

For the Ellesmere MS. I have used the published facsimile, and it is still worth while: it is unlikely that all recent editors would read *this* instead of *the* in l. 182, had not the Chaucer Society's prints, by a slip, given *this* as the Ellesmere reading. Every variation from Ellesmere is recorded in the footnotes. Capitals, pointing, and the distinction of *v* : *u*, *j* : *i* follow modern usage. Where final *-e* must be read as a separate syllable to make up the rhythm, I have printed *è*, except at the end of the line where *-e* is normally syllabic, and in words like *evere* (pronounced *ev/re*) where the alternative *ever* serves for the rhythm. Divergences from the modern English incidence of stress are marked by accents placed over the first vowel of the stressed syllable:—an acute accent when the first or second syllable is stressed, e. g. *óbeisant, coráge*; a grave accent when the third or fourth syllable is stressed, e. g. *creatùre, paciènt*. This method has the advantage of showing that *creatùre* must be read as *cre/a/ture* and *paciènt* as *pa/ci/ent*, each with three syllables.

MATERIALS FOR THE TEXT.

The Ellesmere Chaucer reproduced in facsimile, 2 vols., Manchester, 1911.

Chaucer Society's Publications, Series I, especially

The Six-Text Chaucer (1868-).

The separate prints of *MS. Harley 7334* (1885) and *MS. Cambridge Univ. Dd. 4. 24* (1901-2).

Parallel-Text Specimens, Parts VI and VII: *The Clerk's Tale* (1899-1900), with Koch's Introduction (1902).

Skeat, W. W. *The Works of Geoffrey Chaucer*, 7 vols., Oxford, 1894-7.

Chaucer Society's Publications, Series II, *Originals and Analogues of the Canterbury Tales*, Pt. II (1875). [Contains Petrarch's Latin and Boccaccio's Italian version.]

McCormick, Sir W. *The Manuscripts of Chaucer's Canterbury Tales*, Oxford, 1933.

PORTRAIT OF THE CLERK

General Prologue ll. 285–308

A Clerk ther was of Oxenford also, 285
That unto logyk haddè longe ygo.
As leenè was his hors as is a rake,
And he nas nat right fat, I undertake,
But looked holwe, and therto sobrely.
Ful thredbare was his overeste courtepy, 290
For he hadde geten hym yet no benefice,
Ne was so worldly for to have office:
For hym was levere have at his beddes heed
Twenty bookes, clad in blak or reed,
Of Aristotle and his philosophie, 295
Than robes riche, or fithele, or gay sautrie.
But al be that he was a philosóphre,
Yet hadde he but litel gold in cofre;
But al that he myghte of his freendes hente,
On bookes and on lernynge he it spente, 300
And bisily gan for the soules preye
Of hem that yaf hym wherwith to scoléye.
Of studie took he moost cure and moost heede:
Noght o word spak he moorè than was neede,
And that was seyd in forme and reverence, 305
And short and quyk, and ful of hy senténce;
Sownynge in moral vertu was his speche,
And gladly wolde he lerne, and gladly teche.

Heere folweth the Prologe

OF THE

CLERKES TALE OF OXENFORD.

'SIRE clerk of Oxenford,' oure Hooste sayde,
　'Ye ryde as coy and stille as dooth a mayde,
Were newe spoused, sittynge at the bord; table
This day ne herde I of youre tonge a word:
I trowe ye studie aboute som sophýme; philosophical problem　5
But Salomon seith "every thyng hath tyme."
　For Goddes sake, as beth of bettre cheere!
It is no tyme for to studien heere:
Telle us som myrie tale, by youre fey! See p 45 note
For what man that is entred in a pley　　　　10
He nedes moot unto the pley assente.
But precheth nat, as freres doon in Lente,
To make us for oure olde synnes wepe,
Ne that thy tale make us nat to slepe.
　Telle us som murie strange thyng of áventùres; rhetorical device　15
Youre termes, youre colóurs, and youre figúres,
Keepe hem in stoor, til so be that ye endite compose
Heigh elaborate style, as whan that men to kynges write;
Speketh so pleyn at this tyme, I yow preye,
That we may understonde what ye seye.'　　　20
　This worthy clerk benignely answerde, modestly
'Hooste,' quod he, 'I am under youre yerde: rule

The Clerkes Tale

Ye han of us as now the governance,
And therfore wol I do yow óbeisànce
As fer as resoun axeth, hardily.   25
I wol yow telle a talè which that I
Lerned at Padwe of a worthy clerk,
As preved by his wordes and his werk :
He is now deéd, and nayled in his cheste ;
I prey to God so yeve his soulè reste !   30
    Fraunceys Petràk, the lauriat poéte,
Hightè this clerk, whos rethorikè sweete
Enlúmyned al Ytáille of poetrie,
As Lynyan dide of philosophie,
Or lawe, or oother art particuler ;   35
But Deeth, that wol nat suffre us dwellen heer
But as it were a twynklyng of an eye,
Hem bothe hath slayn, and allè shul we dye.
    But forth to tellen of this worthy man,
That taughtè me this tale, as I bigan,   40
I seye, that first with heigh stile he enditeth,
Er he the body of his talè writeth,
A prohemye in the which discryveth he
Pemond, and of Saluces the contrée,
And speketh of Appenyn, the hilles hye   45
That been the boundes of West Lumbardye,
    And of Mount Vesulus in speciàl,
Where as the Poo out of a wellè smal
Taketh his firstè spryngyng and his sours,
That estward ay encresseth in his cours   50
To Emele-ward, to Férrare, and Venýse :
The which a long thyng werè to devyse ;
And trewèly, as to my juggèment,
Me thynketh it a thyng impertinent,
Save that he wole convoyen his matéere :   55
But this his talè, which that ye may heere.'

31 Perak *Ell*.   32 rethorik *Ell*.   36 suffre us *omitted in Ell*.

Heere bigynneth

THE TALE OF THE CLERK

OF OXENFORD.

THER is at the west syde of Ytáille,
  Doun at the roote of Vesulus the colde,
A lusty playne, habundant of vitáille,
Where many a tour and toun thou mayst biholde   60
That founded were in tyme of fadres olde,
And many another délitáble sighte,
And Sáluces this noble contree highte.

A markys whilom lord was of that lond,
As were hise worthy eldres hym bifore,   65
And óbeisànt and redy to his hond
Were alle hise liges, bothè lasse and moore.
Thus in delit he lyveth, and hath doon yoore,   *a longtira*
Biloved and drad thurgh favour of Fortúne
Bothe of hise lordes and of his commúne.   70

Therwith he was, to speke as of lynáge,
The gentilleste y-born of Lumbardye ;
A fair persóne, and strong, and yong of age,
And ful of honour and of curteisye, *inde*
Discreet ynogh his contree for to gýe,   75
Save in somme thynges he was to blame,
And Walter was this yongè lordes name.

I blame hym thus, that he considereth noght
In tymè comynge what myghte hym bityde,
V.I. But in his lust presént was al his thoght, 80
As for to hauke and hunte on every syde ;
Wel ny alle othere cures leet he slyde ;
And eek he nolde—and that was worst of alle—
Weddè no wyf, for noght that may bifalle.

74 of (1st) *omitted in Ell.*   76 Save . . . he] Save that in somme
thynges that he *Ell.*   79 hym myghte *Ell.*

Oonly that point his peple bar so soore   85
That flokmeele on a day they to hym wente,
And oon of hem, that wisest was of loore,
(Or elles that the lord best wolde assente
That he sholde telle hym what his peple mente,
Or elles koude he shewe wel swich matéere,)   90
He to the markys seyde as ye shul heere:—

'O noble markys, youre humanitee
Asseureth us, and yeveth us hardinesse,
As ofte as tyme is of necessitee,
That we to yow mowe telle oure hevynesse.   95
Accepteth, lord, now, of youre gentillesse,
That we with pitous herte unto yow pleyne,
And lat youre eres nat my voys desdeyne:

Al have I noght to doone in this matéere
Moore than another man hath in this place,   100
Yet for as muche as ye, my lord so deere,
Han alwey shewed me favóur and grace,
I dar the bettre aske of yow a space
Of audiènce to shewen oure requeste;
And ye, my lord, to doon right as yow leste.   105

For certes, lord, so wel us liketh yow
And al youre werk, and evere han doon, that we
Ne koudé nat us-self devysen how
We myghté lyven in moore felicitee,
Save o thyng, lord, if it youre willé be,
That for to been a wedded man yow leste,
Thanne were youre peple in sovereyn hertes reste.

Boweth youre nekke under that blisful yok
Of sovèràynètee, noght of servýse,
Which that men clepeth spousaille or wedlok;   115

93 and yeveth] to yeve *Ell*.   96 of] for *Ell*.   110 it *omitted in Ell.*

And thenketh, lord, among youre thoghtes wyse,
How that oure dayes passe in sondry wyse;
For thogh we slepe or wake, or rome or ryde,
Ay fleeth the tyme, it nyl no man abyde.

And thogh youre grenè youthè floure as yit,   120
In crepeth age alwey, as stille as stoon,
And deeth manáceth every age, and smyt
In ech estaat, for ther escapeth noon;
And also certein as we knowe echoon
That we shul deye, as úncertèyn we alle   125
Been of that day whan deeth shal on us falle.

Accepteth thanne of us the trewe entente
That nevere yet refuseden thyn heeste,
And we wol, lord, if that ye wole assente,
Chese yow a wyf, in short tyme attè leeste,   130
Born of the gentilleste and of the meeste
Of al this land, so that it oghtè seme
Honour to God and yow, as we kan deeme.

Delivere us out of al this bisy drede,
And taak a wyf, for hyè Goddes sake;   135
For if it so bifelle, as God forbede!
That thurgh youre deeth youre lynè sholdè slake,
And that a straungè súccessour sholde take
Youre heritage, O wo were us alyve!
Wherfore we pray yow hastily to wyve.'   140

Hir meekè preyere and hir pitous cheere
Madè the markys hertè han pitee:
'Ye wol,' quod he, 'myn owene peple deere,
To that I nevere erst thoughtè, streynè me.
I me rejoysed of my libertee,   145
That seeldè tyme is founde in mariàge:
Ther I was free, I moot been in serváge.

     145 liberte *Ell.*

But nathèlees I se youre trewe entente,
And truste upon youre wit, and have doon ay ;
Wherfore of my free wyl I wole assente   150
To weddè me, as soone as evere I may ;
But theras ye han profred me today
To chesè me a wyf, I yow relesse
That choys, and prey yow of that profre cesse ;

For God it woot that children oftè been   155
Unlyk hir worthy eldres hem bifore ;
Bountee comth al of God, nat of the streen
Of which they been engendred and y-bore.
I truste in Goddes bontee, and therfore
My mariàge, and myn estaat and reste,   160
I hym bitake,—he may doon as hym leste.

Lat me allone in chesynge of my wyf,—
That charge upon my bak I wole endure ;
But I yow preye, and charge upon youre lyf,
What wyf that I take, ye me assure   165
To worshipe hire, whil that hir lyf may dure,
In word and werk, bothe heere and everywheere,
As she an emperòures doghter weere ;

And forthermoore, this shal ye swere, that ye
Agayn my choys shul neither grucche ne stryve,   170
For sith I shal forgoon my libertee
At youre requeste, as evere moot I thryve !
Ther as myn herte is set, ther wol I wyve.
And but ye wole assente in swich manére,
I prey yow, speketh namoore of this matére.'   175

With hertèly wyl they sworen and assenten
To al this thyng,—ther seydè no wight nay—
Bisekynge hym of grace, er that they wenten,
That he wolde graunten hem a certein day
Of his spousáille, as soone as evere he may ;   180

152 today] this day *Ell.*   154 yow *omitted in Ell.*   174 swich]
this *Ell.*

For yet alwey the peple somwhat dredde
Lest that the markys no wyf woldė wedde.

He grauntèd hem a day, swich as hym leste,
On which he wolde be wedded sikerly,
And seyde he dide al this at hir requeste ; 185
And they with humble ententė, buxomly, *submissively*
Knelynge upon hir knees ful reverently,
Hym thonken alle ; and thus they han an ende
Of hire entente, and hoom agayn they wende.

And heerupon he to hise officères 190
Comaundeth for the festė to purveye,
And to hise privee knyghtes and squiéres
Swich chargė yaf as hym liste on hem leye ;
And they to his comandėment obeye,
And ech of hem dooth al his diligence 195
To doon unto the feestė reverence.

Explicit prima pars.

Incipit secunda pars.

NOGHT fer fro thilkė paleys honuràble
    Wher as this markys shoope his mariàge, *village*
There stood a throopė, of sitė dėlitàble, *plessont*
In which that povre folk of that villáge 200
Hadden hir beestes and hir herbergàge, *dwellings*
And of hire labour tooke hir sustenànce
After that the erthė yaf hem hábundànce.

Amonges thise povre folk ther dwelte a man
Which that was holden povrest of hem alle ; 205
But hyė God somtymė senden kan
His grace into a litel oxes stalle ;
Janicula men of that throope hym calle.
A doghter haddė he, fair ynogh to sighte,
And Grísildis this yongė mayden highte. *was 210
                                          called*

198 Wher] Ther *Ell.*

But for to speke of vertuous beautee,
Thanne was she oon the faireste under sonne;
For povreliche y-fostred up was she,
No likerous lust was thurgh hire herte y-ronne;
Wel ofter of the welle than of the tonne   215
She drank, and for she woldè Vertu plese,
She knew wel labour, but noon ydel ese.

Chaucers addition

But thogh this maydè tendre were of age,
Yet in the brest of hire virginitee
Ther was enclosed rype and sad coráge,   220
And in greet reverence and charitee
Hir oldè povrè fader fostred shee.
A fewè sheepè, spynnynge, on feeld she kepte,
She woldè noght been ydel til she slepte;

And whan she homward cam, she woldè brynge   225
Wortes, or othere herbes, tymes ofte,
The whiche she shredde and seeth for hir lyvynge;
And made hir bed ful harde and nothyng softe;
And ay she kepte hir fadres lyf on-lofte
With everich óbeisàunce and diligence   230
That child may doon to fadres reverence.

Upon Grisilde, this povre creatùre,
Ful oftè sithe this markys sette his eye,
As he on huntyng rood, par áventùre;
And whan it fil that he myghte hire espye,   235
He noght with wantowne lookyng of folýe
Hisè eyen caste on hire, but in sad wyse
Upon hir chiere he wolde hym ofte avyse,

Commendynge in his hertè hir wommanhede,
And eek hir vertu, passynge any wight   240
Of so yong age, as wel in chiere as dede.
For thogh the peple havè no greet insight
In vertu, he considered ful right

211 beautee] bountee *Ell.*   233 sette] caste *Ell.*   235 whan]
whan that *Ell.*   238 wolde] gan *Ell.*   242 have] hadde *Ell.*

Hir bountee, and disposed that he wolde
Wedde hire oonly, if evere he weddė sholde.　　　245

　The day of weddyng cam, but no wight kan
Tellė what womman that it sholdė be ;
For which mervéillė wondred many a man,
And seyden, whan they were in privėtee,
' Wol nat oure lord yet leve his vanytee ?　　　250
Wol he nat wedde ? allas, allas, the while !
Why wole he thus hymself and us bigile ? '

chaucer's addition

　But nathėlees this markys hath doon make
Of gemmes set in gold and in asúre
Brooches and rynges, for Grisildis sake,　　　255
And of hir clothyng took he the mesúre
By a maydė lyk to hire statúre,
And eek of othere äornėmentes alle
That unto swich a weddyng sholdė falle.

The time of undren of the samė day　　　260
Approcheth that this weddyng sholdė be ;
And al the paleys put was in array,
Bothe halle and chambres, ech in his degree ;
Houses of office stuffed with plentee
Ther maystow seen of deyntevous vitáille,　　　265
That may be foundė as fer as last Ytáille.

9 Am

chaucer addition　*extendo*

This roial markys, richėly arrayed,
Lordes and ladyes in his compaignye
The whiche that to the feestė weren y-prayed,
And of his retenue the bachelrye,　　　270
With many a soun of sondry melodye,
Unto the village, of the which I tolde,
In this array the rightė wey han holde.

　　249 whan] whan that *Ell.*　　258 aornementz *Ell.*

Grisilde (of this, God woot, ful innocent,
That for hire shapen was al this array)   275
To fecchen water at a welle is went,
And cometh hoom as soone as ever she may;
For wel she hadde herd seyd that thilkè day
The markys sholdè wedde, and, if she myghte,
She woldè fayn han seyn som of that sighte.   280

She thoghte: 'I wole with othere maydens stonde,
That been my felawes, in oure dore, and se
The markysesse; and therfore wol I fonde
To doon at hoom as soone as it may be
The labour which that longeth unto me,   285
And thanne I may at leyser hire biholde,
If she this wey unto the castel holde.'

And as she wolde over hir thresshfold gon,
The markys cam and gan hire for to calle,
And she set doun hir water-pot anon   290
Biside the thresshfold in an oxes stalle,
And doun upon hir knes she gan to falle,
And with sad contenancè kneleth stille,
Til she had herd what was the lordes wille.

  This thoghtful markys spak unto this mayde   295
Ful sobrely, and seyde in this manére,
'Where is youre fader, O Grísildis?' he sayde;
And she with reverence, in humble cheere,
Answerdè, 'Lord, he is al redy heere:'
And in she gooth, withouten lenger lette,   300
And to the markys she hir fader fette.

He by the hand thanne took this oldè man,
And seydè thus, whan he hym hadde asyde,
'Janicula, I neither may ne kan
Lenger the plesance of myn hertè hyde: 305
If that thou vouchè-sauf, whatso bityde,

277 comth *Ell.*

Thy doghter wol I take, er that I wende,
As for my wyf, unto hir lyves ende.

Thou lovest me, I woot it wel certéyn,
And art my feithful ligè-man y-bore, 310
And all that liketh me, I dar wel seyn,
It liketh thee; and specially therfore
Tel me that poynt that I have seyd bifore,
If that thou wolt unto that purpos drawe
To takè me as for thy sone-in-lawe.' 315

This sodeyn cas this man astonyed so
That reed he wax, abayst, and al quakyng
He stood, unnethes seyde he wordes mo, *hardly*
But oonly thus: 'Lord,' quod he, 'my willynge
Is as ye wole, ne ayeyns youre likynge 320
I wol no thyng, ye be my lord so deere;
Right as yow lust govérneth this matéere.'

'Yet wol I,' quod this markys softely,
'That in thy chambre I and thou and she
Have a collaciòun,—and wostow why? 325
For I wol axe if it hire willè be
To be my wyf, and reule hire after me;
And al this shal be doon in thy presénce,—
I wol noght speke out of thyn audiènce.'

And in the chambre whil they were aboute 330
Hir tretys, which as ye shal after heere, *down*
The peple cam unto the hous withoute,
And wondred hem in how honéste manére
And tentifly she kepte hir fader deere:
But outrely Grisildis wondre myghte, 335
For nevere erst ne saugh she swich a sighte.

No wonder is thogh that she were astoned
To seen so greet a gest come in that place,—
She nevere was to swichè gestes woned, *accustomed*
For which she looked with ful palè face.   340
But, shortly forth this mater for to chace,
Thise arn the wordes that the markys sayde
To this benignè, verray, *true* feithful mayde :—

'Grisilde,' he seyde, 'ye shal wel understonde
It liketh to youre fader and to me   345
That I yow wedde, and eek it may so stonde,
As I suppose, ye wol that it so be.
But thise demandes axe I first,' quod he,
'That (sith it shal be doon in hastif wyse)
Wol ye assente, or elles yow avyse?   350

I seye this: be ye redy with good herte
To al my lust, and that I frely may, *desire*
As me best thynketh, do yow laughe or smerte,
And nevere ye to grucche it, nyght ne day? *complain*
And eek whan I sey "ye" ne sey nat "nay,"   355
Neither by word ne frownyng contenance?
Swere this, and heere I swere oure alliànce.'

Wondrynge upon this word, quakynge for drede,
She seydè, 'Lord, undigne and unworthy
Am I to thilke honóur that ye me beede; *offer*   360
But as ye wole youreself, right so wol I;
And heere I swere that nevere willyngly
In werk ne thoght I nyl yow disobeye,
For to be deed, though me were looth to deye.'

'This is ynogh, Grisildè myn,' quod he,   365
And forth he gooth with a ful sobre cheere
Out at the dore, and after that cam she,
And to the peple he seyde in this manére:
'This is my wyf,' quod he, 'that standeth heere;

337 that *omitted in Ell.*   341 mater] tale *Ell.*   357 oure] yow *Ell.*

Honoureth hire and loveth hire, I preye,   370
Whoso me loveth; ther is namoore to seye.'

And for that nothyng of hir oldè geere
She sholdè brynge into his hous, he bad
That wommen sholde dispoillen hire right theere:
Of which thise ladyes werè nat right glad   375
To handle hir clothes wherinne she was clad—
But nathèlees, this maydè bright of hewe
Fro foot to heed they clothed han al newe.

Hir heris han they kembd, that lay untressed
Ful rudely, and with hir fyngres smale   380
A córone on hire heed they han y-dressed,
And sette hire ful of nowches grete and smale,—
Of hire array what sholde I make a tale?
Unnethe the peple hir knew for hire fairnesse
Whan she translated was in swich richésse.   385

   This markys hath hire spoused with a ryng
Broght for the samè cause, and thanne hire sette
Upon an hors, snow-whit and wel amblyng,
And to his paleys, er he lenger lette,
With joyful peple that hire ladde and mette,   390
Convoyed hire; and thus the day they spende
In revel, til the sonnè gan descende.

And, shortly forth this tale for to chace,
I seye that to this newè markysesse
God hath swich favour sent hire, of his grace,   395
That it ne semed nat, by liklynesse,
That she was born and fed in rudènesse,
As in a cote or in an oxè-stalle,
But norissed in an emperòures halle.

385 translated] transmuted *Corpus MS.*

To every wight she woxen is so deere   400
And worshipful, that folk ther she was bore,
And from hire birthe knewe hire yeer by yeere,
Unnethe trowed they (but dorste han swore)
That to Janicle, of which I spak bifore,
She doghter were, for, as by cónjectùre,   405
Hem thoughte she was another creatùre.

For though that evere vertuous was she,
She was encressed in swich excellence
Of thewes goode, y-set in heigh bountee,
And so discreet and fair of eloquence,   410
So benigne, and so digne of reverence,
And koudé so the peples herte embrace,
That ech hire lovede that looked on hir face.

Noght oonly of Saluces in the toun
Publíced was the bountee of hir name,   415
But eek biside in many a regioun
If oon seide wel, another seyde the same;
So spradde of hire heighé bountee the fame
That men and wommen, as wel yonge as olde,
Goon to Saluce upon hire to biholde.   420

Thus Walter lowely—nay! but roially—
Wedded with fortunat honéstétee,
In Goddes pees lyveth ful esily
At hoom, and, outward, grace ynogh had he;
And for he saugh that under low degree   425
Was ofté vertu hid, the peple hym heelde
A prudent man, and that is seyn ful seelde.

Nat oonly this Grisildis thurgh hir wit
Koude al the feet of wyfly homlynesse,
But eek, whan that the cas required it,   430
The commune profit koudé she redresse:

404 That] That she *Ell.*   405 were] nas *in some MSS.*
415 bountee] beautee *Ell.*   418 fame] name *Ell.*   425 low]
heigh *Ell.*   426 ofte *omitted in Ell.*   429 humblenesse *Ell.*

Ther nas discórd, rancóur, ne hevynesse
In al that land that she ne koude apese,
And wisely brynge hem alle in reste and ese.

Though that hire housbonde absent were anon,   435
If gentil men or othere of hire contrée
Were wrothe, she woldè bryngen hem at-on. *reconcile them*
So wise and rypè wordes haddè she,
And juggèmentz of so greet equitee,
That she from hevene sent was, as men wende,   440
Peple to save, and every wrong t' amende.

   Nat longè tyme after that this Grisild
Was wedded, she a doghter hath y-bore,
Al had hire levere have born a knavè-child; *she would rather*
Glad was this markys and the folk therfore,   445
For though a maydè-child coome al bifore,
She may unto a knavè-child atteyne,
By liklihede, syn she nys nat baréyne.

Explicit secunda pars.

Incipit tercia pars.

THER fil, as it bifalleth tymes mo, *short while*
   Whan that this child had souked but a throwe,   450
This markys in his hertè longeth so
To tempte his wyf, hir sadnesse for to knowe,
That he ne myghte out of his hertè throwe
This merveillous desir his wyf t' assaye :
Nedelees, God woot, he thoghte hire for t' affraye.   455

He hadde assayed hire ynogh bifore,
And foond hire evere good ; what neded it *changes*
Hire for to tempte, and alwey moore and moore ? *views*
Though som men preise it for a subtil wit,
But as for me, I seye that yvele it sit   460
To assaye a wyf whan that it is no nede,
And putten hire in angwyssh and in drede.

444 knave-] man- *Ell.*   447 knave-] man- *Ell.*

                                     C

For which this markys wroghte in this manére:
He cam allone a-nyght ther as she lay,
With stiernè face and with ful trouble cheere,   465
And seydè thus: 'Grisilde,' quod he, 'that day
That I yow took out of youre povere array
And putte yow in estaat of heigh noblésse,
Ye have nat that forgeten, as I gesse?

I seye, Grisilde, this present dignitee   470
In which that I have put yow, as I trowe
Maketh yow nat foryetful for to be
That I yow took in povre estaat, ful lowe
For any wele ye moot youreselven knowe.
Taak heede of every word that y yow seye,—   475
Ther is no wight that hereth it but we tweye.

Ye woot yourself wel how that ye cam heere
Into this hous, it is nat longe ago;
And though to me that ye be lief and deere,
Unto my gentils ye be nothyng so: 480
They seyn to hem it is greet shame and wo
For to be subgetz and been in serváge
To thee, that born art of a smal villáge;

And namely sith thy doghter was y-bore
Thise wordes han they spoken, doutèlees.   485
But I desire, as I have doon bifore,
To lyve my lyf with hem in reste and pees;
I may nat in this caas be recchèlees:
I moot doon with thy doghter for the beste,
Nat as I wolde, but as my peple leste.   490

.And yet, God woot, this is ful looth to me;
But nathèlees, withoutè youre wityng
I wol nat doon; but this wol I,' quod he,
'That ye to me assente as in this thyng.
Shewe now youre paciènce in youre werkyng   495

482 and] and to *Ell.*

That ye me highte and swore in youre villáge
That day that maked was oure mariàge.'

    Whan she had herd al this, she noght ameved
Neither in word or chiere or contenaunce ;
For, as it semed, she was nat agreved.   500
She seydè, ' Lord, al lyth in youre plesáunce ;
My child and I with hertèly óbeisàunce
Been youres al, and ye mowe save and spille
Youre owene thyng : werketh after youre wille.

Ther may no thyng, God so my soulè save,   505
Liken to yow that may displesè me,
Ne I ne desirè no thyng for to have,
Ne dredè for to leese, save oonly thee ;
This wyl is in myn herte, and ay shal be ;
No lengthe of tyme, or deeth, may this deface,   510
Ne chaungè my coráge to another place.'

    Glad was this markys of hire answeryng,
But yet he feyned as he were nat so :
Al drery was his cheere and his lookyng
Whan that he sholde out of the chambre go.   515
Soone after this, a furlong wey or two,
He privèly hath toold al his entente
Unto a man, and to his wyf hym sente.

A maner sergeant was this privee man,
The which that feithful ofte he founden hadde   520
In thynges grete, and eek swich folk wel kan
Doon execucìoun on thynges badde ;
The lord knew wel that he hym loved and dradde ;
And whan this sergeant wiste his lordes wille,
Into the chambre he stalked hym ful stille.   525

'Madame,' he seyde, 'ye moote foryeve it me
Though I do thyng to which I am constreyned;
Ye been so wys that ful wel knowe ye
That lordes heestes mowe nat been y-feyned;
They mowe wel been biwailled or compleyned,   530
But men moote nede unto hire lust obeye,
And so wol I—ther is namoore to seye—

This child I am comanded for to take:'
And spak namoore, but out the child he hente
Despitously, and gan a cheere make   535
As though he wolde han slayn it er he wente.
Grisildis moot al suffren and consente,
And as a lamb she sitteth meke and stille,
And leet this crueel sergeant doon his wille.

Suspecious was the diffame of this man,   540
Suspect his face, suspect his word also,
Suspect the tyme in which he this bigan.
Allas! hir doghter that she loved so
She wende he wolde han slawen it right tho;
But nathelees she neither weepe ne syked,   545
Conformynge hire to that the markys lyked.

But atte laste speken she bigan,
And mekely she to the sergeant preyde,
So as he was a worthy gentil man,
That she moste kisse hir child er that it deyde;   550
And in hir barm this litel child she leyde,
With ful sad face, and gan the child to blisse,
And lulled it, and after gan it kisse.

And thus she seyde in hire benigne voys:
'Fareweel, my child, I shal thee nevere see;   555
But sith I thee have marked with the croys,
Of thilke Fader blessed moote thou be
That for us deyde upon a croys of tree.

530 or] and *Ell.*   546 Conformynge] Consentynge *Ell.*   547 to speken
Ell.   552–3 blisse . . . kisse] kisse . . . blisse *Ell.*   557 thou] he *Ell.*

Thy soulė, litel child, I hym bitake,
For this nyght shaltow dyen for my sake.'   560

I trowe that to a norice in this cas
It had been hard this reuthe for to se ;
Wel myghte a mooder thanne han cryd 'allas!'
But nathėlees so sad-stidefast was she
That she endured al adversitee,   565
And to the sergeant mekėly she sayde,
'Have heer agayn youre litel yongė mayde :'

'Gooth now,' quod she, 'and dooth my lordes heeste ;
But o thyng wol I prey yow, of youre grace,
That, but my lord forbad yow, attė leeste   570
Burieth this litel body in som place
That beestes ne no briddes it to-race.
But he no word wol to that purpos seye,
But took the child and wente upon his weye.

This sergeant cam unto his lord ageyn,   575
And of Grisildis wordes and hire cheere
He tolde hym point for point, in short and pleyn,
And hym presenteth with his doghter deere.
Somwhat this lord hath routhe in his manére ;
But nathėlees his purpos heeld he stille,   580
(As lordes doon whan they wol han hir wille)

And bad his sergeant that he pryvėly
Sholdė this child softė wynde and wrappe
With allė circumstances tendrely,
And carie it in a cofre or in a lappe ;   585
But, upon peyne his heed of for to swappe,
That no man sholdė knowe of his entente,
Ne whenne he cam, ne whider that he wente ;

564 sad-stidefast] sad and stidefast *Ell.*   588 he cam *omitted in*
Ell.

But at Boloignè to his suster deere,
That thilkè tyme of Panik was countesse,   590
He sholde it take, and shewe hire this matéere,
Bisekynge hire to doon hire bisynesse
This child to fostre in allè gentillesse ;
And whos child that it was he bad hire hyde
From every wight, for oght that may bityde.   595

    The sergeant gooth, and hath fulfild this thyng :
But to this markys now retournè we,
For now gooth he ful faste, ymaginyng
If by his wyves cheere he myghtè se,
Or by hire word apérceyvè, that she   600
Were chaunged ; but he nevere hire koudè fynde
But evere in oon y-likè sad and kynde.

As glad, as humble, as bisy in servýse
And eek in love, as she was wont to be,
Was she to hym in every maner wyse,   605
Ne of hir doghter noght a word spak she :
Noon accident for noon adversitee
Was seyn in hire, ne nevere hir doghter name
Ne nempned she, in ernest nor in game.

Explicit tercia pars.

Sequitur pars quarta.

IN this estaat ther passed been foure yeer   610
    Er she with childè was ; but, as God wolde,
A knavè-child she bar by this Walter,
Ful graciòus and fair for to biholde ;
And whan that folk it to his fader tolde,
Nat oonly he, but al his contree, merye   615
Was for this child, and God they thanke and herye.

590 Pavik *Ell.*   594 hire] hym *Ell.*   612 knave-] man- *Ell.*

Whan it was two yeer old, and fro the brest
Departed of his norice, on a day
This markys caughtè yet another lest
To tempte his wyf yet ofter, if he may.　　　620
O, nedelees was she tempted in assay!
But wedded men ne knowè no mesúre,
Whan that they fynde a pacient creatùre.

'Wyf,' quod this markys, 'ye han herd er this
My peple sikly berth oure mariàge,　　　625
And namely sith my sone y-boren is,
Now is it worse than evere in al oure age.
The murmure sleeth myn herte and my corráge,
For to myne eres comth the voys so smerte,
That it wel ny destroyed hath myn herte.　　　630

Now sey they thus: "Whan Walter is agon,
Thanne shal the blood of Janicle succede,
And been oure lord, for oother have we noon."
Swiche wordes seith my peple, out of drede:
Wel oughte I of swich murmur taken heede,　　　635
For certeinly I dredè swich senténce,
Though they nat pleyn speke in myn audiènce.

I woldè lyve in pees, if that I myghte;
Wherfore I am disposed outrely,
As I his suster servedè by nyghte,　　　640
Right so thenke I to serve hym pryvély.
This warne I yow, that ye nat sodeynly
Out of youreself for no wo sholde outreye:
Beth paciènt, and therof I yow preye.'

'I have,' quod she, 'seyd thus, and evere shal— 645
I wol no thyng, ne nyl no thyng, certayn,
But as yow list; naught greveth me at al
Though that my doughter and my sone be slayn—
At youre comandèment, this is to sayn;
I have noght had no part of children tweyne　　　650
But first siknesse, and after wo and peyne.

626 yborn *Ell*.　　　640 served *Ell*.

Ye been oure lord: dooth with youre owene thyng
Right as yow list; axeth no reed at me;
For as I lefte at hoom al my clothyng
Whan I first cam to yow, right so,' quod she, 655
'Lefte I my wyl and al my libertee,
And took youre clothyng: wherfore, I yow preye,
Dooth youre plesáunce; I wol youre lust obeye.

And certes, if I haddè prescience
Youre wyl to knowe er ye youre lust me tolde, 660
I wolde it doon withouten necligence.
But now I woot youre lust and what ye wolde,
Al youre plesáncè ferme and stable I holde;
For wiste I that my deeth wolde do yow ese,
Right gladly wolde I dyen yow to plese: 665

Deth may noght makè no comparisoun
Unto oure love!' And whan this markys say
The constance of his wyf, he caste adoun
Hise eyen two, and wondreth that she may
In paciéncè suffre al this array; 670
And forth he goth with drery contenance,
But to his herte it was ful greet plesánce.

 This ugly sergeant, in the samè wyse
That he hire doghter caughtè, right so he
(Or worsè, if men worsè kan devyse,) 675
Hath hent hire sone, that ful was of beautee:
And evere in oon so paciènt was she
That she no chierè maade of hevynesse,
But kiste hir sone, and after gan it blesse.

Save this: she preyede hym that, if he myghte, 680
Hir litel sone he wolde in erthè grave,
His tendre lymes, delicaat to sighte,
Fro foweles and fro beestes for to save.
But she noon answere of hym myghtè have,—

He wente his wey, as hym nothyng ne roghte;   685
But to Boloigne he tendrely it broghte.

This markys wondreth evere lenger the moore
Upon hir paciènce, and if that he
Ne haddè soothly knowen ther-bifoore
That parfitly hir children loved she,   690
He wolde have wend that of som subtiltee,   *supposed*
And of malíce, or for crueel coráge,
That she hadde suffred this with sad viságe.

But wel he knew that, next hymself certáyn,
She loved hir children best in every wyse.   695
But now of wommen wolde I axen fayn
If thise assayes myghtè nat suffise?
What koude a sturdy housbonde moore devyse
To preeve hir wyfhod and hir stedefastnesse,
And he continuynge evere in sturdinesse?   700

But ther been folk of swich condicíoun
That, whan they have a certein purpos take,
They kan nat stynte of hire entencíoun,
But, right as they were bounden to a stake,
They wol nat of that firstè purpos slake.   705
Right so this markys fulliche hath purpósed
To tempte his wyf, as he was first disposed.

He waiteth if by word or contenance
That she to hym was changed of coráge,
But nevere koude he fyndè variance: 710
She was ay oon in herte and in viságe;
And ay the forther that she was in age,
The moorè trewe—if that it were possíble—
She was to hym in love, and moore penýble.   *anxious to please*

687 wondred *Ell.*   699 and] or *Ell.*   704 a] that *Ell.*

For which it semed thus, that of hem two   715
Ther nas but o wyl ; for, as Walter leste,
The same lust was hire plesánce also ;
And, God be thanked ! al fil for the beste.
She shewed wel, for no worldly unreste
A wyf, as of hirself, nothing ne sholde   720
Wille in effect, but as hir housbonde wolde.

The sclaundre of Walter ofte and wyde spradde,
That of a crueel herte he wikkedly,
For he a povre womman wedded hadde,
Hath mordred bothe his children privèly—   725
Swich murmure was among hem comunly :
No wonder is, for to the peples ere
Ther cam no word but that they mordred were.

For which, whereas his peple ther-bifore
Hadde loved hym wel, the sclaundre of his diffame   730
Made hem that they hym hatede therfore :
To been a mordrere is an hateful name.
But nathèlees, for ernest ne for game,
He of his crueel purpos nolde stente :
To tempte his wyf was set al his entente.   735

Whan that his doghter twelf yeer was of age,
He to the court of Rome, in subtil wyse
Enformed of his wyl, sente his messáge,
Comaundynge hem swiche bulles to devyse
As to his crueel purpos may suffyse,   740
How that the pope, as for his peples reste,
Bad hym to wedde another, if hym leste.

I seye, he bad they sholde countrefete
The popes bulles, makynge menciòun
That he hath leve his firstè wyf to lete,   745
As by the popes dispensaciòun,
To styntè rancour and dissenciòun

731 hated *Ell.*

Bitwixe his peple and hym—thus seyde the bulle,
The which they han publíced attè fulle.

   The rudè peple, as it no wonder is,   750
Wenden ful wel that it hadde be right so ;
But whan thise tidynges cam to Grísildis,
I deemè that hire hertè was ful wo.
But she, y-likè sad for everemo,
Disposed was, this humble creatùre,   755
The adversitee of Fortune al t' endure,

Abidynge evere his lust and his plesánce
To whom that she was yeven, herte and al,
As to hire verray worldly súffisànce.
But, shortly if this storie I tellen shal,   760
This markys writen hath in speciàl
A lettre in which he sheweth his entente,
And secreely he to Boloigne it sente :

To the erl of Panyk, which that haddè tho
Wedded his suster, preyde he specially   765
To bryngen hoom agayn hise children two
In honuràble estaat, al openly ;
But o thyng he hym preyede outrely,
That he to no wight, though men wolde enquere,
Sholdè nat telle whos children that they were,   770

But seye, the mayden sholde y-wedded be
Unto the markys of Saluce anon.
And as this erl was preyed, so dide he ;
For at day set he on his wey is goon
Toward Saluce, and lordes many oon,   775
In riche array, this mayden for to gyde,
Hir yongè brother ridynge hire bisydè.

Arrayed was toward hir mariàge
This fresshė maydė, ful of gemmes cleere;
Hir brother, which that seven yeer was of age,   780
Arrayed eek ful fressh in his manére.
And thus in greet noblésse, and with glad cheere,
Toward Saluces shapynge hir journéy,
Fro day to day they ryden in hir wey.

Explicit quarta pars.

Sequitur pars quinta.

AMONG al this, after his wikke uságe,   785
This markys, yet his wyf to temptė moore
To the outtrestė preeve of hir coráge,
Fully to han experience and loore
If that she were as stidefast as bifoore,
He on a day in open audiènce   790
Ful boistously hath seyd hire this senténce :—

'Certes, Grisilde, I hadde ynogh plesánce
To han yow to my wyf, for youre goodnesse,
As for youre trouthe and for youre óbeisànce—
Noght for youre lynage ne for youre richésse;   795
But now knowe I, in verray soothfastnesse,
That in greet lordshipe, if I wel avyse,
Ther is greet servitute in sondry wyse.

I may nat doon as every plowman may;
My peple me constreyneth for to take   800
Another wyf, and crien day by day;
And eek the popė, rancour for to slake,
Consenteth it, that dar I undertake;
And treweliche, thus muche I wol yow seye,
My newė wyf is comynge by the weye.   805

Be strong of herte, and voyde anon hir place,
And thilkè dowere that ye broghten me
Taak it agayn,—I graunte it of my grace ;
Retourneth to youre fadres hous,' quod he ;
' No man may alwey han prosperitee ;   810
With evene herte I redè yow t' endure
The strook of Fortune or of áventùre.'

    And she agayn answerde in paciènce,
' My lord,' quod she, ' I woot, and wiste alway,
How that bitwixen youre magnificence   815
And my povértè, no wight kan ne may
Maken comparisoun, it is no nay.
I ne heeld me nevere digne in no manére
To be youre wyf, no, ne youre chamberère.

And in this hous ther ye me lady maade,   820
The heighè God take I for my witnesse,
And also wysly he my soulè glaade,
I nevere heeld me lady ne maistresse,
But humble servant to youre worthynesse,
And evere shal, whil that my lyf may dure,   825
Aboven every worldly creatùre.

That ye so longe, of youre benignitee,
Han holden me in honour and nobléye,
Where as I was noght worthy for to bee,
That thonke I God and yow, to whom I preye   830
Foryelde it yow ; ther is namoore to seye.
Unto my fader gladly wol I wende,
And with hym dwelle unto my lyves ende.

  812 The] This *Ell.*   813 answerde agayn *Ell.*   819 chambrere
Ell.   829 for to *omitted in Ell.*

Ther I was fostred of a child ful smal,
Til I be deed my lyf ther wol I lede,   835
A wydwe clene in body, herte, and al;
For sith I yaf to yow my maydenhede,
And am youre trewe wyf, it is no drede,   *undoubtedly*
God shilde swich a lordes wyf to take   *forbid*
Another man to housbonde or to make!   *mate*   840

And of youre newe wyf God, of his grace,
So graunte yow wele and prosperitee;
For I wol gladly yelden hire my place,
In which that I was blisful wont to bee;
For sith it liketh yow, my lord,' quod shee,   845
'That whilom weren al myn hertes reste,
That I shall goon, I wol goon whan yow leste.

But theras ye me profre swich dowáire
As I first broghte, it is wel in my mynde
It were my wrecched clothes, nothyng faire,   850
The whiche to me were hard now for to fynde.   •
O goode God! how gentil and how kynde
Ye semed by youre speche and youre viságe
The day that maked was oure mariàge!

But sooth is seyd, algate I fynde it trewe—   855
For in effect it preeved is on me—
Love is noght oold as whan that it is newe.
But certes, lord, for noon adversitee,
To dyen in the cas, it shal nat bee
That evere in word or werk I shal repente   860
That I yow yaf myn herte in hool entente.

My lord, ye woot that in my fadres place
Ye dide me streepe out of my povre weede,
And richely me cladden, of youre grace.
To yow broghte I noght elles, out of drede,   *respect*   865
But feith and nakednesse and maydenhede;
And heere agayn my clothyng I restoore,
And eek my weddyng ryng, for everemoore.

The remenant of youre jueles redy be
Inwith youre chambre, dar I saufly sayn :   870
Naked out of my fadres hous,' quod she,
' I cam, and naked moot I turne agayn.
Al youre plesánce wol I folwen fayn :
But yet I hope it be nat youre entente
That I smoklées out of youre paleys wente.   875

Ye koude nat doon so díshonèste a thyng,
That thilké wombe, in which youre children leye,
Sholdé biforn the peple in my walkyng
Be seyn al barè ; wherfore, I yow preye,
Lat me nat lyk a worm go by the weye.   880
Remembre yow, myn owene lord so deere,
I was youre wyf, though I unworthy weere.

Wherfore, in gerdoun of my maydenhede, *recompense*
Which that I broghte, and noght agayn I bere,
As voucheth sauf to yeve me, to my meede,   885
But swich a smok as I was wont to were,
That I therwith may wrye the wombe of here
That was youre wyf : and heer take I my leeve
Of yow, myn owene lord, lest I yow greve.'

' The smok,' quod he, ' that thou hast on thy bak, 890
Lat it be stille, and bere it forth with thee.'
But wel unnethes thilké word he spak,
But wente his wey, for routhe and for pitee. *Compassion*
Biforn the folk hirselven strepeth she,
And in hir smok, with heed and foot al bare,   895
Toward hir fader hous forth is she fare.

The folk hire folwe, wepynge in hir weye,
And Fortune ay they cursen as they goon ;
But she fro wepyng kepte hire eyen dreye,
Ne in this tymé word ne spak she noon.   900
Hir fader, that this tidynge herde anoon,
Curseth the day and tymé that natúre
Shoope hym to been a lyves creatùre.

For, out of doute, this oldė povre man
Was evere in suspect of hir mariàge,   905
For evere he demed, sith that it bigan,
That whan the lord fulfild hadde his coráge,
Hym woldė thynke it were a dísparàge
To his estaat so lowė for t' alighte,
And voyden hire as soone as ever he myghte.   910

Agayns his doghter hastiliche goth he,
For he by noyse of folk knew hire comynge,
And with hire oldė coote, as it myghte be,
He covered hire, ful sorwėfully wepynge ;
But on hire body myghte he it nat brynge ;   915
For rudė was the clooth, and moore of age
By dayes fele, than at hire mariàge.

Thus with hire fader for a certeyn space
Dwelleth this flour of wyfly paciènce,
That neither by hire wordes ne hire face,
Biforn the folk, ne eek in hire absénce,   920
Ne shewed she that hire was doon offence ;
Ne of hire heighe estaat no rémembràunce
Ne haddė she, as by hire contenàunce.

No wonder is, for in hire grete estaat   925
Hire goost was evere in pleyn humylitee :
No tendre mouth, noon hertė delicaat,
No pompė, no semblánt of roialtee,
But ful of paciènt benyngnytee,
Discreet and pridėlees, ay honuràble,   930
And to hire housbonde evere meke and stable.

Men speke of Job, and moost for his humblesse,
As clerkes, whan hem list, konne wel endite,
Namely of men ; but as in soothfastnesse,
Though clerkes preisė wommen but a lite,   935
Ther kan no man in humblesse hym acquite

916 and] and she *Ell.*

As wommen kan, ne kan been half so trewe
As wommen been,—but it be falle of-newe.

[Explicit quinta pars.

Sequitur pars sexta.]

FRO Boloigne is this erl of Panyk come,
Of which the fame upsprang to moore and lesse,
And in the peples eres, alle and some,   941
Was kouth eek that a newe markysesse
He with hym broghte, in swich pompe and richésse,
That nevere was ther seyn with mannes eye
So noble array in al West Lumbardye.   945

The markys, which that shoope and knew al this,
Er that this erl was come, sente his messáge
For thilke sely povre Grísildis;
And she with humble herte and glad viságe,
Nat with no swollen thoght in hire coráge,   950
Cam at his heste, and on hire knees hire sette,
And reverently and wisely she hym grette.

'Grisilde,' quod he, 'my wyl is outrely
This mayden, that shal wedded been to me,
Received be tomorwe as roially   955
As it possíble is in myn hous to be;
And eek that every wight in his degree
Have his estaat in sittyng and servýse
And heigh plesáunce, as I kan best devyse.

I have no wommen súffisaunt, certayn,   960
The chambres for t'arraye in ordinaunce
After my lust, and therfore wolde I fayn
That thyn were al swich manere governaunce;
Thow knowest eek of old al my plesáunce:
Thogh thyn array be badde and yvel biseye,   965
Do thou thy devoir, at the leeste weye.'

937 As ... been] As womman kan ne been *Ell.*   939 Pavyk *Ell.*

'Nat oonly, lord, that I am glad,' quod she,
'To doon youre lust, but I desire also
Yow for to serve and plese in my degree
Withouten feyntyng, and shal everemo ;   970
Ne nevere, for no welė ne no wo,
Ne shal the goost withinne myn hertė stente
To love yow best, with al my trewe entente.'

And with that word she gan the hous to dighte,
And tables for to sette, and beddes make,   975
And peyned hire to doon al that she myghte,
Preyynge the chamberères for Goddes sake
To hasten hem, and fastė swepe and shake ;
And she, the moostė servysable of alle,
Hath every chambre arrayed and his halle.   980

Abouten undren gan this erl alighte,
That with hym broghte thise noble children tweye,
For which the peple ran to seen the sighte
Of hire array, so richėly biseye ;
And thanne at erst amonges hem they seye   985
That Walter was no fool thogh that hym leste
To chaunge his wyf, for it was for the beste.

For she is fairer, as they deemen alle,
Than is Grisilde, and moorė tendre of age,
And fairer fruyt bitwene hem sholdė falle,   990
And moorė plesant, for hire heigh lynáge ;
Hir brother eek so fair was of viságe,
That hem to seen the peple hath caught plesáunce,
Commendynge now the markys governaunce.

Auctor. 'O stormy peple, unsad and evere untrewe !
Ay undiscreet, and chaungynge as a vane,   996
Delitynge evere in rumbul that is newe,
For lyk the moone ay wexė ye and wane ;
Ay ful of clappyng, deere ynogh a jane ;

977 chambreres *Ell.*

Youre doom is fals, youre constance yvele preeveth :
A ful greet fool is he that on yow leeveth !'   1001

Thus seyden saddè folk in that citee,
Whan that the peple gazed up and doun,
For they were glad, right for the noveltee,
To han a newè lady of hir toun.   1005
Namoore of this make I now menciòun,
But to Grisilde agayn wol I me dresse,
And telle hir constance and hir bisynesse.

    Ful bisy was Grisilde in everythyng
That to the feestè was apertinent ;   1010
Right noght was she abayst of hire clothyng,
Thogh it were rude and somdeel eek to-rent,
But with glad cheerè to the yate is went,
With oother folk, to greete the markysesse,
And after that dooth forth hire bisynesse.   1015

With so glad chiere hise gestes she receyveth,
And konnyngly, everich in his degree,
That no defautè no man áperceyveth ;
But ay they wondren what she myghtè bee
That in so povre array was for to see,   1020
And koudè swich honóur and reverence ;
And worthily they preisen hire prudénce.

In al this meenè-whilè she ne stente
This mayde and eek hir brother to commende
With al hir herte, in ful benyngne entente,   1025
So wel that no man koude hir pris amende :
But attè laste, whan that thise lordes wende
To sitten doun to mete, he gan to calle
Grisilde, as she was bisy in his halle.

    1013 is] is she *Ell.*   1017 konnyngly] so konnyngly *Ell.*

'Grisilde,' quod he, as it were in his pley,　　1030
'How liketh thee my wyf and hire beautee?'
'Right wel,' quod she, 'my lord, for, in good fey,
A fairer saugh I nevere noon than she.
I prey to God yeve hire prosperitee,
And so hope I that he wol to yow sende　　1035
Plesánce ynogh, unto youre lyves ende.

O thyng biseke I yow and warne also,
That ye ne prikkè with no tormentynge
This tendre mayden, as ye han doon mo;
For she is fostred in hire norissynge　　1040
Moore tendrely, and, to my súpposynge,
She koudè nat adversitee endure
As koude a povre-fostred creatùre.'

And whan this Walter saugh hire paciènce,
Hir gladè chiere, and no malíce at al,　　1045
And he so ofte had doon to hire offence,
And she, ay sad and constant as a wal,
Continuynge everè hire innocence overal,
This sturdy markys gan his hertè dresse
To <u>rewen</u> upon hire wyfly stedfastnesse.　　1050

'This is ynogh, Grisildè myn,' quod he,
'Be now namoore agast, ne yvele apayed;
I have thy feith and thy benyngnytee,
As wel as evere womman was, assayed,
In greet estaat, and povreliche arrayed;　　1055
Now knowe I, dere wyf, thy stedfastnesse'—
And hire in armes took and gan hire kesse.

And she, for wonder, took of it no keepe;
She herdè nat what thyng he to hi　scyde;
She ferde as she had stert out of a　eepe,　　1060
Til she out of hir mazednesse abra　le.
Grisilde quod he, by God that　us dyde!

1045 glad *Ell.*　1046 offence *omitted ..　Ell.*　1056 dere]
goode *Ell.*

Thou art my wyf, ne noon oother I have,
Ne nevere hadde, as God my soulè save!

   This is thy doghter which thou hast supposed   1065
To be my wyf; that oother, feithfully,
Shal be myn heir, as I have ay purpósed:
Thou bare hym in thy body trewèly.
At Boloigne have I kept hem privèly:
Taak hem agayn, for now maystow nat seye   1070
That thou hast lorn noon of thy children tweye?

And folk that ootherweys han seyd of me,
I warne hem wel that I have doon this deede
For no malíce, ne for no crueltee,
But for t' assaye in thee thy wommanheede,   1075
And nat to sleen my children, God forbeede!
But for to kepe hem pryvèly and stille,
Til I thy purpos knewe and al thy wille.'

   Whan she this herde, aswownè doun she falleth
For pitous joye; and after hire swownynge   1080
She bothe hire yongè children to hire calleth,
And in hire armes, pitously wepynge,
Embraceth hem, and tendrely kissynge
Ful lyk a mooder, with hire saltè teeres
She bathed bothe hire visage and hire heeres.   1085

   O, which a pitous thyng it was to se
Hir swownyng, and hire humble voys to heere!
' Grauntmercy, lord, that thanke I yow,' quod she,
'That ye han saved me my children deere.
Now rekke I nevere to been deed right heere: 1090
Sith I stonde in youre love and in youre grace,
No fors of deeth, ne whan my spirit pace

1063 ne *om* ... *d i.* ...   1067 ...
1081 to] unto ... *ill.* ... 1088 Grauntmercy ...
many MSS.

O tendre, O deere, O yongė children myne!
Youre woful mooder wendė stedfastly
That crueel houndes or som foul vermýne   1095
Hadde eten yow; but God, of his mercy,
And youre benyngnė fader, tendrely
Hath doon yow kept;' and in that samė stounde
Al sodeynly she swapte adoun to grounde.

And in hire swough so sadly holdeth she   1100
Hire children two, whan she gan hem t' embrace,
That with greet sleighte and greet difficultee
The children from hire arm they gonne arace.
O! many a teere on many a pitous face
Doun ran of hem that stooden hire bisyde;   1105
Unnethe abouten hire myghte they abyde.

Walter hire gladeth and hire sorwe slaketh;
She riseth up abaysed from hire traunce,
And every wight hire joye and feestė maketh,
Til she hath caught agayn hire contenaunce.   1110
Walter hire dooth so feithfully plesáunce
That it was deyntee for to seen the cheere
Bitwixe hem two, now they been met y-feere.

    Thise ladyes, whan that they hir tymė say,
Han taken hire and into chambre gon,   1115
And strepen hire out of hire rude array,
And in a clooth of gold that brightė shoon,
With a coróune of many a richė stoon
Upon hire heed, they into halle hire broghte,
And ther she was honúred as hire oghte.   1120

Thus hath this pitous day a blisful ende,
For every man and womman dooth his myght
This day in murthe and revel to dispende,
Til on the welkne shoon the sterres lyght.
For moore solémpne in every mannes syght   1125
This festė was, and gretter of costáge,
Than was the revel of hire mariàge.

Ful many a yeer in heigh prosperitee
Lyven thise two in concord and in reste;
And richèly his doghter maryed he   1130
Unto a lord, oon of the worthieste
Of al Ytáille; and thanne in pees and reste
His wyves fader in his court he kepeth,
Til that the soule out of his body crepeth.

His sone succedeth in his heritage   1135
In reste and pees after his fader day,
And fortunat was eek in mariàge—
Al putte he nat his wyf in greet assay:
This world is nat so strong, it is no nay,
As it hath been in oldè tymes yoore,   1140
And herkneth what this auctour seith therfoore:—

This storie is seyd, nat for that wyves sholde
Folwen Grisilde as in humylitee,
For it were ínportàble, though they wolde;
But for that every wight in his degree   1145
Sholdè be constant in adversitee
As was Grisildè: therfore Petrak writeth
This storie, which with heigh stile he enditeth.

For sith a womman wàs so paciènt
Unto a mortal man, wel moore us oghte   1150
Receyven al in gree that God us sent,
For greet skile is, he preevè that he wroghte.
But he ne tempteth no man that he boghte,
As seith Seint Jame, if ye his pistel rede;
He preeveth folk al day, it is no drede,   1155

And suffreth us, as for oure excercise,
With sharpè scourges of adversitee
Ful oftè to be bete in sondry wise,
Nat for to knowe oure wyl, for certes he
Er we were born knew al oure frelètee;   1160
And for oure beste is al his governaunce.
Lat us thanne lyve in vertuous suffráunce.

1140 in] of *Ell.*   1160 al *omitted in Ell.*

But o word, lordynges, herkneth er I go :—
It were ful hard to fyndė nowadayes
In al a toun Grisildis thre or two ;　　　　　1165
For, if that they were put to swiche assayes,
The gold of hem hath now so badde alayes
With bras, that thogh the coyne be fair at eye,
It woldė rather breste a-two than plye.

For which heere, for the Wyves love of Bathe,　1170
Whos lyf and al hire sectė God mayntene
In heigh maistrie—and elles were it scathe—
I wol with lusty hertė fressh and grene
Seyn yow a song to gladė yow, I wene,
And lat us stynte of ernestful matére.　　　　1175
Herkneth my song, that seith in this manére :—

Lenvoy de Chaucer.

GRISILDE is deed, and eek hire paciènce,
　And bothe at ones buryed in Ytáille,
For which I criė in open audiènce
No wedded man so hardy be t' assaille　　　　1180
His wyves paciènce, in hope to fynde
Grisildis, for in certein he shal faille.

O noble wyves, ful of heigh prudénce,
Lat noon humylitee youre tongė naille,
Ne lat no clerk have cause or diligence　　　　1185
To write of yow a storie of swich merváille
As of Grisildis, paciènt and kynde,
Lest Chichivache yow swelwe in hire entráille.

Folweth Ekko, that holdeth no silénce,
But evere answereth at the countretaille !　　1190
Beth nat bidaffed for youre innocence,
But sharply taak on yow the governaille.
Emprenteth wel this lessoun in youre mynde
For commune profit, sith it may availle :

Ye archiwyves, stondeth at defense !   1195
Syn ye be strong as is a greet camáille,
Ne suffreth nat that men yow doon offense.
And sklendre wyves, fieble as in batáille,
Beth egre as is a tygre yond in Ynde,
Ay clappeth as a mille, I yow consáille: 1200

Ne dreed hem nat, doth hem no reverence ;
For though thyn housbonde armed be in maille,
The arwes of thy crabbed eloquence
Shal perce his brest and eek his áventàille.
In jalousie I rede eek thou hym bynde,   1205
And thou shalt make hym couche as doth a quaille.

If thou be fair, ther folk been in presénce
Shewe thou thy visage and thyn ápparàille ;
If thou be foul, be fre of thy dispence,
To gete thee freendes ay do thy travàille ;   1210
Be ay of chiere as light as leef on lynde,
And lat hym care, and wepe, and wrynge, and waille.

Heere endeth

the Tale of the Clerk

of Oxenford

The Clerkes Tale

[Bihoold the murye wordes of the Hoost.

This worthy clerk whan ended was his tale,
Oure hoostè seyde, and swoor by Goddes bones,
' Me were levere than a barel ale
My wyf at hoom had herd this legende ones ;
This is a gentil talè for the nones,   [5]
As to my purpos, wistè ye my wille,—
But thyng that wol nat be, lat it be stille.']

[2] hoost *Ell.*

The Prologe of the Marchantes tale.

'Wepyng and waylyng, care and oother sorwe,
I knowe ynogh, on even and a-morwe,'
Quod the Marchant, 'and so doon othere mo   1215
That wedded been—I trowe that it be so,
For wel I woot it fareth so with me.
I have a wyf, the worsté that may be,
For thogh the feend to hire y-coupled were,
She wolde hym overmacche, I dar wel swere.   1220
What sholde I yow reherce in speciàl
Hir hyè malíce?   She is a shrewe at al.
Ther is a long and largè difference
Bitwix Grisildis gretè paciènce
And of my wyf the passyng crueltee.   1225
Were I unbounden, also moot I thee!
I woldè nevere eft comen in the snare.
We wedded men lyven in sorwe and care;
Assayè who so wole, and he shal fynde
I seyè sooth, by seint Thomas of Ynde!—   1230
As for the moorè part, I sey nat alle:
God shildè, that it sholdè so bifalle!

A, goode Sire Hoost, I have y-wedded bee
Thise monthes two, and moorè nat, pardee;
And yet, I trowè, he that al his lyve   1235
Wyflees hath been, though that men wolde him ryve
Unto the herte, ne koude in no manère
Tellen so muchel sorwe as I now heere
Koude tellen of my wyves cursednesse!'

'Now,' quod oure hoost, 'Marchant, so God yow blesse,
Syn ye so muchel knowen of that art,   1241
Ful hertèly I pray yow telle us part.'
'Gladly,' quod he, 'but of myn owenè soore,
For soory herte, I tellè may namoore.'

1228 lyve *Ell.*

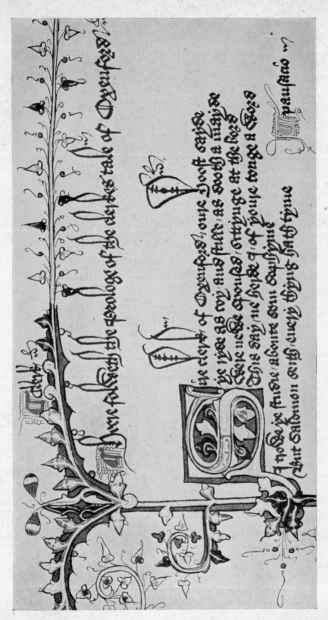

The beginning of *The Clerkes Prologue* in the Ellesmere MS.

NOTES

General Prologue

PROL. 285. *A Clerk ther was of Oxenford also* : A clerk was either an official of the Church, or (as here) one prepared by his education to undertake the duties of an ecclesiastic. Chaucer's Clerk was probably quite a young man, and neither preferment in the Church, nor a secular office for which his learning would fit him, had yet come his way. No doubt he belonged to a poor family ; for there were many such ready to make heavy sacrifices to give their sons the benefits of learning. For them the Church was the only way to social advancement ; but it was a crowded way ; and pleasant manners, a good voice, and a pretty taste in music, seem to have been better credentials than poverty and devotion to philosophy. It is interesting to compare Chaucer's description of a more frivolous Oxford clerk, the 'hendė Nicholas' of the *Miller's Tale* :

> His Almageste, and *bookes grete and smale*,
> His astrelabie longynge for his arte,
> His augrym-stones, layen faire apart
> On shelves, couched *at his beddes heed* :
> His presse y-covered with a faldyng reed :
> And all above ther lay *a gay sautrie*,
> On which he made a-nyghtes melodie . . .
> And thus this sweetė clerk his timė spente
> *After his freendes fyndynge* and his rente.

Nicholas professed an inclination to the science of astrology. *Almageste* is the Arab name of the great work of Ptolemy on astronomy ; *augrym-stones* are counters to help in calculation ; and the *astrelabie* is that astronomical instrument whose intricacies Chaucer expounded in a prose treatise to 'litel Lowis his sone', at 'the tendre age of ten yeer'.

PROL. 287-8. In the Ellesmere portrait, which is reproduced (reversed) at the head of the Text, the horse's ribs show up well : but the Clerk himself is plump enough ; and the attempt to portray his studious expression fails so dismally that he looks a simpleton.

PROL. 294. *clad in blak or reed* : best taken as a tag of the kind quoted in the note to l. 9 (iv) below, for red is the type of

43

colour, black of its absence.   The meaning is 'of all forms' or at most 'in any kind of cover'; cp. *Hous of Fame* ii. 566 ff.:

> Whan any speche y-comen is
> Up to the paleys, anon-right
> Hit wexeth lyk the samè wyght
> Which that the word in erthè spak,
> Be he *clothed reed or blak*.

I fancy the Clerk's books were tatterdemalions, not sumptuous volumes in red and black morocco.   Observe that in the account of Nicholas quoted above, *bookes* is followed by just such a tag; and again in the *Prologue to the Legend of Good Women, Version A,* 273 f. where the God of Love chides Chaucer:

> Yis, God wot, *sixty bokys, olde and newe,*
> Hast thow thyself, alle ful of storyes grete . . .,

whence we gather also that *twenty* is but a round number.

PROL. 297–8 : i.e. his study of philosophy had not brought him the philosopher's stone which transmutes base metals to gold. Chaucer gives a picture of the mediaeval alchemist in his Canon's Yeoman's *Prologue* and *Tale*.

PROL. 301. *And bisily gan for the soules preye,*
    Of hem that yaf hym wherwith to scoléye.

A remarkable readiness to pay for prayers meets us everywhere in the fourteenth century; and many clerks lived on it long after their days of study were past.   See what professes to be an autobiographical passage by the author of *Piers Plowman*, C-Text, vi. 36 ff.

> 'Wanne ich yong was', quath ich, 'meny yer hennes,
> My fader and my frendes founden me to scole . . .
> And ich lyve in Londene and on Londen bothe;
> The lomes ['tools'] that ich laboure with, and lyflode deserve,
> Is *Paternoster,* and my Prymer, *Placebo* and *Dirige,*
> And my Sauter som tyme, and my Sevene Psalmes:
> Thus ich synge for hure soules of suche as me helpen.'

PROL. 303. *studie* : 'deep thought'—he was a thinker rather than a talker.   We can still say 'in a brown study'.

The Clerkes Tale

2–3 'You ride as shy and tongue-tied as is a maid just married, sitting at table.'   With the whole passage compare the words of the Host to the Clerk in the *Prologue* 840 f., when he calls on the pilgrims to draw for the honour of telling the first tale :   And ye, sire Clerk, lat be your shamfastnesse:
    Ne studieth noght.

were newè spoused = that were newe spoused : note the rather common ellipse of the relative in Middle English, and the device by which Modern English avoids the subjunctive.

6 *Salomon seith* : 'To everything there is a season', Ecclesiastes iii. 1.

7 *as beth* = 'be'. This use of *as* to introduce an imperative has not been recorded outside of Chaucer's work, where there are several examples, e.g. *As voucheth sauf to yeue me ... swich a smok* 885. It appears to be a polite softening of the imperative, and to spring from the use of *so, as, also* in phrases expressing a wish like :

> I prey to God *so* yeve his soulè reste.   l. 30.

> And of youre newè wyf God, of his grace,
> *So* grauntè yow wele and prosperitee.   ll. 841–2.

So is used with an imperative in *The Man of Law's Tale* 861 :

> And if thou darst nat saven hym, for blame,
> *So kys* hym ones in his fadres name.

9 *by youre fey* : one of many stock phrases which made riming easy. Classical and modern taste reject them ; but Chaucer, the near successor of the minstrels who gave them their vogue, uses them freely, not only in his Tales, where the habits of unstudied spoken verse are appropriate, but in his formal poetry. It is worth while to read the text with an eye for such rime-making tags, which fall into rough classes: (i) affirmations, e.g. *as evere moot I thryve* 172 ; *God so my soulè save!* 505, 1064 : *that dar I undertake* 803 ; *dar I saufly sayn* 870 ; and the kindred *doutelees* 485 ; *out of drede* 634, 865 ; *it is no drede* 838, 1155 ; *it is no nay* 1139. (ii) Another class promises speedy progress in the tale, e.g. ll. 39-40, and the repeated *But, shortly forth this talè for to chace* 341, 393, cp. 760 ; or introduces important matter, e.g. This his talè, *which that ye may heere* 56, cp. 91, 331 ; or cuts a speech short, *ther is namoore to seye* 371, 532, 831, cp. 1006. (iii) Some are adverbial, e.g. *As soone as evere (she) may* 151, 180, 277, cp. 284 ; *withouten lenger lette* 300, cp. 389. (iv) An important group of circumlocutions for 'all', 'everything', &c., depends on the collocation of two words of opposite sense : *lasse and moore* 67, 940 ; *grete and smale* 382 ; *alle and some* 941 ; *as wel yonge as olde* 419 ; *in ernest nor in game* 609, 733 ; *nyght ne day* 354 ; *laughe or smerte* 353 ; and so on. Failure to notice that these tags do not bear the full literal meaning of their component words sometimes leads to misinterpretation ; see note to l. 609.

10 f. i.e. 'Whoever joins in a game must conform to its rules'. Skeat points out that this renders the Old French proverb *Ki*

en jeu entre, jeu consente. The rules of the competition in tale-telling are laid down near the end of the *Prologue*, and when he calls on a pilgrim for his tale, the Host commonly refers to their compact.

12 *But precheth nat, as freres doon in Lente.* The popularity of the friars (as distinct from the monks) was largely due to the attention they gave to preaching. The Host does not want his company to be harrowed on this journey by a Lenten call to repentance; for he at least regarded the pilgrimage to St. Thomas as a holiday, not a penance. It is hard to imagine him in sackcloth and ashes.

14 *Ne that . . . nat.* Note the change of construction. Render 'and let not'. An accumulation of negatives in Middle English merely emphasizes the negation; see for instance ll. 971–3:

> *Nè* nevere, for *no* welè *ne no* wo,
> *Ne* shal the goost withinne myn herte stente
> To love yow best . . .

16 *termes—colóurs—figúres*: cp. *Hous of Fame* ii. 346 ff., where the Eagle prides himself on his simple explanation of the passage of news to Fame's house:

> Have I not preved thus symply,
> Withouten any subtilitee
> Of speche, or gret prolixitee
> Of termes of philosophye,
> Of figures of poetrye,
> Or colóurs of rethorike?
> Pardee! Hit oghtè thee to lyke,
> For hard langáge and hard matére
> Is encombrous for to here
> At ones: wost thou not wel this?

18 *Heigh style*: a style so elaborate as to be hard to understand: cp. l. 41 and note to l. 1148. In the *Squire's Tale* 105 ff. the address of the Knight of the brazen horse to King Cambyuskan is introduced by a pun on the phrase:

> Al be it that I kan nat sowne his stile,
> Ne kan nat clymben over so heigh a style,
> Yet seye I this, as to commúne entente,
> Thus muche amounteth al that evere he mente.

22 *under youre yerde* is paraphrased in the next line: the *yerde* or rod is the symbol of authority; cp. *Parlement of Foules* 639 ff.:

> Myn rightful lady, goddesse of Natúre,
> Soth is that I am evere under your yerde,
> Like as is everich other creatùre.

46

25 'As far as reason demands, assuredly', i. e. 'within reason'—a prudent reservation.

27 *at Padwe.* To Petrarch was sometimes given Livy's local name 'Patavinus', 'of Padua', because from 1368 till his death in 1374 he lived chiefly at Padua, or in his country house at Arqua near by. It is not surprising that Chaucer should associate Petrarch with the town, or should imply that the Clerk had visited a University so famous in the Middle Ages, and so much sought by English students.

of a worthy clerk: Petrarch was an ecclesiastic by profession

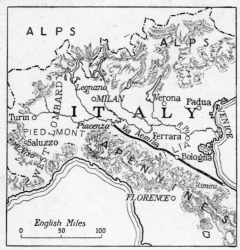

—he was archdeacon of Padua and canon of Parma—and so is properly called a *clerk*.

31 *Petrak*: a correct form. His father's name was Petracco, a diminutive of Pietro 'Peter'. The poet's true name was Francesco di Petracco, 'Francis, son of Petracco'; but this he changed to the more dignified Francesco Petrarca.

the lauriat poëte: Petrarch, who was eager to revive interest in classical studies, and besides, not a little vain of his own accomplishment, was ambitious to be publicly crowned with the poet's bays, as Virgil and Horace had been. By 1340 his European fame was such that both the Roman Senate and the

University of Paris offered him that honour. He naturally preferred Rome, and, as a preliminary, stood a public examination before King Robert of Naples. In 1341 he was crowned with laurel in the Capitol, amid great pomp.

33 *of poetrie . . . of philosophie*: 'with poetry . . . with philosophy'.

34 *Lynyan*: Giovanni di Legnano (d. 1383) was so called from his birthplace, Legnano (see map). He taught Canon Law at Bologna, and enjoyed some fame as a philosopher in his own time, when 'philosophy' had a wider meaning than it has now. Since l. 38 refers to his death, the Prologue to *The Clerkes Tale* in its present form must be dated after 1383.

44 ff. *Pemond*: 'Pie(d)mont', the district between the Alps and the Apennines, is so named because it lies at the 'feet of the mountains'. *Saluces*: the marquisate of which Saluzzo is the capital. *Mount Vesulus*: Mount Viso, the highest peak (12,600 feet) in the Cottian Alps, and, from its permanent snow, called 'the colde' in l. 58.

48 *Where as*: 'where'. Cp. 829 (note) and 464 (note) for the use of *as* to form compound conjunctions.

51 *To Emele-ward*, 'towards Emilia'. Observe that Chaucer can still at his convenience write either *toward Caunterbury* Prologue 27, or *to Caunterbury-ward* Prologue 793. The group of provinces still called Emilia included those served by the *Via Aemilia*, a military road from Piacenza to Rimini which is named after its designer, M. Aemilius Lepidus, consul 187 B.C. *Férrare* is the province of which Ferrara is capital. *Venýse*, the state, rather than the town of Venice.

56 *But this his talè*: this ellipse of *is* is fairly common in Middle English ; cp. *Havelok* 606 :

'Goddot !' quath Grim, 'þis ure eir' ('this is our heir').

58 *at the roote of Vesulus*: the first recorded instance in English of the usage 'root' (of a mountain). It comes from Petrarch's Latin *ad radicem Vesuli*.

76 An awkward line to scan. Some MSS. insert *that* after *Save*, some after *thynges*. Modern editors prefer the latter. But the MS. evidence points rather to

Sáve | in sómme | thýnges | he wás | to blám|e

as original. *Somme*, though plural, is not disyllabic in Chaucer.

78–81 'I blame him for this, that he did (*lit.* does) not consider what might happen to him in the future ; but all his thoughts were upon his present pleasures, such as hawking and hunting all about.' *lust presént*: note the post-position of the adjective, which is imitated from French.

85 *Oonly that point* : 'that point alone', i.e. his unwillingness to marry.

97 'the complaint we make with heavy hearts'; *that* = 'that which'; cp ll. 144, 546.

99-105 This stanza is an expansion of: *non quod singulare aliquid habeam ad hanc rem, nisi quod tu me inter alios charum tibi multis indiciis comprobasti.*

99 *Al have I noght to doone*, &c. ; 'Although I am not more concerned in this matter than anybody else present.'

105 *as yow leste* : 'as it may please you'. One of the features that distinguish Middle English syntax from modern is the free use of impersonal verbs with the dative; e.g. *leste, liste* (subjunctive), *list, lust* (contracted 3 sg. pres. indic. = *lusteth*) 'it please(s)' 111, 183, 193, 322, 647, 653, 742, 847; *lyketh* 'it pleases' 312, 345, 845; *thynketh* 'it seems' 54, 353, 908. So long as the dative is a pronoun with a form distinct from the nominative, e. g. dat. *yow* beside nom. *ye*, these constructions are clear ; but when the dative is a noun, it tends to be treated as a nominative, and the verb to become personal, e.g. *as my peple leste* 490 ; *as Walter leste* 716 ; *to that the markys lyked* 546 (note). For other impersonal constructions see notes to ll. 106, 444, 685, 1120.

106 *us liketh yow* : lit. 'it pleases us in respect of you.' *liketh* impers. here has exceptionally two datives, *us* and *yow*.

112 *in sovereyn hertes reste* : 'in supreme peace of mind'.

121 *as stille as stoon* : an old tag which Keats transmuted into 'quiet as a stone'. Other alliterative phrases are : *word and werk* word and deed' 28, 167 ; *tour and toun* 60 ; *rome or ryde* 118 ; *stalked stille* 525 ; *as light as leef on lynde* 1211. But Chaucer, living in a great age of alliterative poetry, does not make much use of alliteration. Perhaps he despised it as provincial. Certainly, when his 'rime doggerel' of *Sir Thopas* is cut short by the Host, he does not take up the suggestion :

Lat se wher thou kanst tellen aught in geeste,

(i.e. 'let us see whether you can tell us anything in alliterative verse') ; but prefers prose for his second attempt, the *Tale of Melibeus*. His Parson too ranks alliterative verse a little below rime, and tells his tale in prose :

But trusteth wel, I am a southren man,
I kan nat geeste 'rum, ram, ruf' by lettre,
Ne, God woot, rym holde I but litel bettre.

122 *smyt* : contracted 3 sg. pres. indic. = *smiteth*. See Note on Chaucer's language, § 8, note (*c*).

127 *of us the trewe entente, That*, &c. : 'the true wish of us

who', &c. Note the inversion to secure a rime; similar are *of Saluces the contrée* 44; *of Saluces in the toun* 'in the town of Saluces' 414; *of my wyf the passyng crueltee* Merchant's *Prologue* (1225).

130 *in short tyme atte leeste:* 'as soon as possible', 'with the least possible delay'.

134 *bisy drede:* 'incessant fear'—a fear that occupies the mind continually.

142 *the markys hertè:* note how Chaucer handled a problem that is still with us—how to form the genitive of a word of which the nominative ends in *s*; cp. *for Grisildis sake* 255; *Grisildis wordes* 576.

144 'constrain me to ⟨do⟩ that ⟨which⟩ I never before purposed ⟨to do⟩.'

162 *in chesynge of my wyf:* 'in the choosing of my wife'; *chesynge* is a verbal noun = 'choice'.

165 *What wyf that I take:* 'whatever wife I take.'

174–5 Not expressed in the Latin.

195 *dooth al his diligence:* 'does his utmost endeavour.' Phrases of similar meaning are: *doon hire bisynesse* 592; *dooth his myght* 1122; *do thy travâille* 1210.

203 *After that:* 'according as'.

212 *oon the faireste:* this construction with the superlative, common in Middle English, is still found occasionally in Shakespeare's time; e.g. *Henry VIII* II. iv. 48 f. 'one the wisest prince'. But the modern form 'one *of* the fairest' is found already in Chaucer, e.g. *oon of the worthieste* 1131.

213 'Because she was poorly nurtured, no luxurious pleasure had touched (lit. penetrated) her heart.' When Dekker collaborated with Chettle and Haughton to write the play of *Patient Grissill* (1603), he celebrated Griselda's simple life in the song beginning:

Art thou poore, yet hast thou golden Slumbers?
    Oh sweet content!
Art thou rich, yet is thy minde perplexed?
    Oh punnishment!
Dost thou laugh to see how fooles are vexed
To ad to golden numbers golden numbers?
    O sweet content, O sweet content!

215–17: Chaucer's addition. 'She drank more often from the spring than from the wine-cask'; but this is understatement: he means that she drank no strong drink.

219 *in the brest of hire virginitee:* 'in her virgin breast'.

221–31 Here is Petrarch's Latin:

Patris senium inestimabili refovens charitate, et pauculas eius oves pascebat, et colo interim digitos atterebat; vicissimque domum rediens, oluscula et dapes fortunae congruas praeparabat; durumque cubiculum sternebat; et ad summam, angusto in spatio, totum filialis obedientiae ac pietatis officium explicabat.
Boccaccio simply says they were very poor.

227 *hir lyvynge*: '*their* sustenance'.

242 *the peple*: people of common intelligence, people generally: cp. Petrarch: *et virtutem eximiam supra sexum supraque aetatem, quam vulgi oculis conditionis obscuritas abscondebat, acri penetrarat intuitu.*

249–52 Chaucer's expansion.

253 *hath doon make*: 'has caused (people) to make', 'has had made'; a regular Middle English use of 'do' with the active infinitive. For *don* in the same sense used with the participle, see l. 1098.

258 *äornêmentes*: I do not know why editors reject the rarer form in favour of the easier reading *ornementes*. The scansion is probably: And éek | of óth|r äór|nemént|es áll|e.
Othere is a spelling for *othre*, of which final *e* is elided before the following vowel.

260 f. 'The mid-morning of the day fixed for the wedding is at hand'; *hora iam prandii aderat* (Petrarch). At l. 981 *abouten undren* translates *hora tertia*, i.e. about 9 a.m.

264–6 Chaucer's addition.

264 *Houses of office*: 'domestic offices', larders, pantry, &c.

266 *as fer as last Ytáille*: 'as far as Italy extends'; i.e. the farthest corners of Italy had been searched for delicacies. *last*: contracted 3 sg. pres. indic. = *lasteth*.

274–94 Based on: *Griseldis, omnium quae erga se pararentur ignara, peractis quae agenda domi erant, aquam e longinquo fonte convectans, paternum limen intrabat, ut expedita curis aliis ad visendam domini sui sponsam cum puellis comitibus properaret.*

287 'If she take this way to the castle.'

289 *gan hire for to calle*: 'called her'. *gan* (pl. *gonne* 1103) is commonly used with the infinitive to form a simple preterite with no inchoative meaning. So at ll. 292, 535, 552, 553, 679, 981, 1028, 1049, 1057, 1101, where 'begin' makes bad sense.

297 Scan: Where is | youre fád|r o Grí|sildis | he sáyd|e.

313 f. 'Declare to me the matter I have already spoken of—whether you will agree', &c. In Petrarch the direct request of ll. 314–15 comes upon Janicula quite unprepared. Chaucer, by broaching the subject in ll. 304–8, gives him more time to think, and weakens the effect of ll. 316 ff.

327 *and reule hire after me*: 'and order her life according to my wishes.'

346 *it may so stonde*, &c.: 'it may well be, I think, that you desire that it should be so.'

349 f. *That . . . Wol ye assente*: *assent, consent* (e.g. l. 803) sometimes take a direct object, and to construe *that* as the direct object here is perhaps easier than to assume a violent break in the construction.

358–64 Petrarch has: *Ad haec illa, miraculo rei tremens, 'Ego, mi domine, (inquit) tanto honore me indignam scio: at si voluntas tua, sique sors mea est, nil ego unquam sciens, nedum faciam, sed etiam cogitabo, quod contra animum tuum sit: nec tu aliquid facies, etsi me mori iusseris, quod moleste feram.'* These are fine sentiments for a simple peasant girl. Contrast Boccaccio: *A cui ella rispose, 'Signor mio, sì',* 'And she answered, "Yes, my lord."'

364 *For to be deed*: i. e. though obedience involve my death: see the Latin above; and *Knight's Tale* 275:

> nevere, for to dyen in the peyne,
> Neither of us in love to hyndre oother.

375 f. *Of which thise ladyes were nat right glad*, &c.: This touch of realism is Chaucer's own; cp. 916 f., where again he goes beyond his original. In refinement of taste he falls behind Petrarch.

380 *hir fyngres smale*: '*their* slim fingers'.

381 *A córone*: a wedding garland? Or a coronet, as in l. 1118?

390 *ladde*: 'accompanied'; *mette* refers to those who came out from the town to meet the procession.

403–5 I have retained the best supported MS. reading *were* in l. 405 by taking *but dorste han swore* as an aside, thrown in to make the rime, and meaning 'but durst have sworn (the contrary)'. Some MSS. have *nas*, but this may be a patching of a difficult original. Modern editors read *nas* or *nere*.

412 'And had such power to grip the people's affections.'

416 *biside*: 'round about'.

422–4 The received text of Petrarch reads: *Sic Gualtherus humili quidem, sed insigni ac prospero matrimonio honestatis summa domi in pace, extra vero summa cum gratia hominum, vivebat.* This was certainly the text before Chaucer, and it is copied into the margin of the Ellesmere MS. But *honestatis* is awkward. Some MSS. omit it. Hendrickson, *Modern Philology* iv. 191 suggests *honestatus.*

424 The Latin brings out the contrast between *at hoom* 'in his own household', and *outward* 'among the people'.

427 *and that is seyn ful seelde*: a tag to fill out the verse. It is hard to say whether it means: (i) 'and hidden virtue is seldom discerned', *or* (ii) 'and such discernment is rare', *or* (iii) 'and such recognition by the people of a ruler's discernment is rare'. The first is least likely; the last is to be preferred.

429 'Knew all the practice of a wife's domestic duties': *feet* 'act', is the modern *feat,* from Old French *fet,* Latin *factum. homlynesse*: this, the reading of the Corpus (Oxford) and Lansdowne MSS., has been rightly preferred by modern editors to *humblenesse* which is found in most of the MSS. The Latin is: *Neque vero solers sponsa muliebria tantum haec domestica, sed, ubi res posceret, publica etiam obibat officia.*

444 'Although she would rather have had a boy.' *Al had hire levere* is a confusion of two constructions: (i) the verb 'to be' with the dative pronoun, which goes back to Old English:—*hire were leuere,* 'it would have been preferable to her'; (ii) the verb 'to have' with the nominative pronoun as subject, which first appears in early Middle English:— *she had leuere,* 'she had rather'. *Had hire leuere* combines the dative pronoun of (i) with the verb of (ii).

449 'It happened, as it sometimes does happen.' *tymes mo*: lit. 'more times', 'at other times'. The rimes of the first five lines of this stanza are forced.

452 *To tempte his wyf*: 'to test', 'to prove' = *assaye* below: and so at ll. 458; but at l. 1153 it has the modern sense 'induce to sin'.

455 *he thoghte hire for t'affraye*: 'he purposed to alarm her'; but *affraye* is stronger, rather 'to destroy her peace of mind by fears'.

460–2 Chaucer's own comment; *yvele it sit*: 'it ill becomes (a husband)'; *sit* contracted 3 sg. pres. indic. = *sitteth*. The sense 'to be fitting' is borrowed from the cognate Old French *set,* 3rd sg. pres. indic. (Lat. *sedet*).

464 *ther as she lay*: 'to where she lay'; to her chamber.

473 f. *ful lowe,* &c.: i. e. 'very humble, if one considers what small measure of good fortune it was in your own power to enjoy'. *For* here has the vague meaning of our 'as regards'.

508 *save oonly thee*: the Ellesmere MS. reads *thee* vel *yee,* and so does the closely related Hengwrt MS. Of the others, some have *thee,* some *yee*: the variants arise because in Chaucer's time *save* is followed either by the nominative or the objective case. Most editors prefer *yee,* since the plural

is the more usual form of respectful address; but *thee* may well be Chaucer's, following the Latin *nisi te*; and we cannot be sure that the alternative *yee* is his correction.

511 Simply 'nor deflect me (from my duty)'. We can still say a person's 'heart is in its right place'.

516 *a furlong wey or two*: 'in a little while'. In Middle English measures of length are often used as measures of time, e. g. *Floris and Blauncheflur* 929 f.

> Here kissinge i-laste a mile
> And þat hem þuʒte litel while.

(Their kissing lasted 'a mile', yet it didn't seem long to them.) The bridge between the original and the transferred sense is 'the time it takes to go a furlong', &c. Shakespeare has 'one inch of delay' *As You Like It* III. ii. 206.

519 *A maner sergeant*: 'a sort *of* attendant'. Old English has a phrase of the type *þrēora cynna* (gen. pl.) *dēor* 'animals of three kinds', which in Middle English, by loss of the genitive inflexion, becomes *thre kyn deer*. As the French *maner(e)* was equivalent to *kin* in some senses, it often took the same construction: *thre maner men*, &c., beside the normal *thre maner of men*. Similarly *every maner wyse* 605; *al swich manere governaunce* 963.

525 *he stalked hym ful stille*: 'he stepped very softly'— no doubt to heighten Griselda's fears: cp. ll. 540 ff.
hym: with a verb of motion the dative pronoun is often used reflexively in Old and Middle English: e. g. *as I me rode*.

534–9 Petrarch has only: *sermone abrupto, quasi crudele ministerium silentio exprimens, subticuit.*

540 *Suspecious was the diffame*, &c. This touch of rhetoric is from Petrarch: *Suspecta viri fama, suspecta facies, suspecta hora, suspecta erat oratio*, &c.

542 *Suspect the tyme*: it was at night—a time for dark deeds; cp. l. 464. The Marquis took some pains to create an atmosphere of terror for his experiment.

546 *Conformynge*: the Ellesmere reading *consentynge* is passable; but it is supported by only one MS. (Hodson) of little value, and seems to depend on a misreading: *confo(u)rmynge* may be written *confo'mynge*, and in scripts of the time *f* and *ſ* (= *s*), *o* and *e*, *m* and *nt*, are like enough to be confused if the curl representing the *ur* missed a copyist's eye.
to that the markys lyked: 'to that which was pleasing to the Marquis'; cp. note to l. 105.

547–60 The matter of these two stanzas is Chaucer's own.

552 f. *blisse . . . kisse*: I have altered the Ellesmere order

kisse . . . blisse with hesitancy, for it is intrinsically good, and has the support of l. 679 below. But it is hard to dispose of the evidence, not merely of the Corpus and Harley 7334 traditions, but of Hengwyrt and nearly all MSS. of the Ellesmere group, that *blisse . . . kisse* is Chaucer's order, and that the Ellesmere order is an editorial improvement modelled on l. 679. The alternative is to assume, whenever it suits our taste, that Ellesmere (or any other chosen MS.) has been corrected quite exceptionally by reference to a superior tradition now lost. There is, it is true, a reason why an original *kisse . . . blisse* might be altered:—*blisse* here = *blesse* in the sense 'to mark with the sign of the cross'—see l. 556; but if it were understood as *blisse* 'to make glad' it would seem awkward after *lulled it*. In a twelfth-century sermon printed in Morris and Skeat's *Specimens Pt. I*, p. 3, we find: 'What does a mother do to her child? *First* she cheers it and gladdens (*blissið*) it by the light, and *afterwards* puts it under her arm or covers its head to make it sleep and rest.' But the appearance of such an alteration in nearly all MSS. is not easily explained.

557 *thou*: it is possible, but not commendable, to defend the Ellesmere MS. reading *he*, by pointing:

> But sith I thee have marked with the croys
> Of thilkè Fader (blessed moote He be!)
> That for us deyde upon a croys of tree,
> Thy soulè, litel child, I Hym bitake.

560 *for my sake*: 'on my account'—the Marquis has explained that Griselda's humble birth was the cause of discontent among his people (ll. 479 ff. above).

567 *youre litel yongè mayde*: there is something juridical in Grisilda's consistency. She renounces all share in the child because she holds that it is the Marquis's to dispose of; cp. 502-4; 650-3.

570 f. *That ... Burieth*: a broken construction; *that* should be followed by a clause with verb in the subjunctive; but *burieth* is the imperative.

579 'This lord shows some signs of compassion.'

581 Chaucer's comment.

584 'tenderly, with every attention'.

588 *whenne*: 'whence'(OE. *hwanon*). In the Ellesmere MS. it is glossed *unde*, so that already in the fifteenth century the risk of misunderstanding was felt.

590 *Panik*: *Panago* in Boccaccio; *Panicum* in Petrarch; but the place, if it ever existed, has not been identified. The Ellesmere scribe writes it clearly *Pavik*, a form which results from confusion of *u* and *n* in scripts of the time.

602 *evere in oon*: 'always, without change'; cp. 677 and 711; *in oon* 'in one and the same state' is a variant form of *anon*, OE. *on ān* 'in one'.

609 *in ernest nor in game*: 'on any occasion', see note to l. 9 (iv). Mr. Pollard in his note to the Globe edition *ad loc.* says the rendering is unhappy; but the literal meaning 'seriously or in jest' was not in Chaucer's mind.

621–3 Chaucer's addition.

625 *sikly berth*: a direct translation of the Latin *aegre ferre*.

628 *sleeth myn herte and my coráge*: 'smites with affliction my heart and mind'; cp. *Franklin's Tale* 165:

This rokkes sleen myn hertè for the feere.

667 *oure love*: is the reading of the Corpus (Oxford) MS., which is typical of a group of MSS. that diverge from the Ellesmere. *youre love* (Ellesmere MS.) probably means '⟨my⟩ love of you'; but Petrarch has *nec mors ipsa nostro fuerit par amori*.

685 *as hym nothyng ne roghte*: 'as if it mattered nothing to him', 'as if he cared not at all'. For the impersonal *roghte*, pa. t. of *rekketh* 'it recks', see note to l. 105.

687 *evere lenger the moore*: 'ever the longer the more'; 'more and more as time goes on'.

693 *That* is redundant.

696–700 It is Chaucer who calls on women to judge of the Marquis's conduct. His style is more familiar and conversational than Petrarch's, who has: *Poterant rigidissimo coniugi haec benevolentiae et fidei coniugalis experimenta sufficere.*

700 'While he himself persisted in his harshness.'

701–7 Petrarch has: *Sed sunt qui ubi semel inceperint non desinant, immo incumbant, haereantque proposito.*

708 *He waiteth*: 'he watches'—the common early meaning; *wait* (borrowed into English from the Norman equivalent of modern French *guetter*) is derived from the same Germanic root as our *wake* and *watch*.

if . . . That: 'if'.

719–21 'She showed well ⟨by her example⟩ that, of her own initiative, a wife should not, on account of any worldly ⟨cause of⟩ unrest, desire anything, except what her husband desires.'

724 *For*: 'because'.

731 *Made hem that they hym hatedè therfore*: 'made them hate him for it'.

738 *messáge*: 'messengers' rather than 'message': cp. *Man of Law's Tale* 333: *Goddes message, Makomete,* 'Mahomet, God's messenger'.

56

741 *How that* : ' to the effect that '.

759 ' to be her solace in this world '.

774 *at day set* : ' on the appointed day '.

811-12 Chaucer's addition.

822 *And also wysly he my soule glaade*, &c. : ' and as surely as He may give my soul joy . . . ', i. e. ' and I swear by my hope of salvation '.

826 *Aboven every worldly creature* : a loose phrase, to be construed closely with *youre worthynesse* above, which is itself a formal periphrasis for *you*, like ' your worship '. The sense is ' I regard myself as servant to *you above all others* '.

829 *Where as* : ' where ', ' in a rank in which ', cp. l. 48 note.

830   *That thonke I God and yow, to whom I preye*
       Foryelde it yow :
' and I pray to Him to requite you for it.' The coupling of God and the Marquis, which reads oddly now, is found also in ll. 133, 1096 f.

834 f. *Ther I was fostred of a child*, &c. : ' Where I was nurtured from earliest childhood, there will I lead my life until I die.'

837-40 Not in Petrarch.

838 *it is no drede* : ' undoubtedly ' ; lit. ' there is no fear (of the contrary) ' ; see note to l. 9.

850 *It were my wrecched clothes* : with *it* used to anticipate a plural subject, the verb is regularly in the plural in Middle English, e. g. *Hous of Fame* iii. 231 ff. *pursevauntes and heraudes . . . Hit weren alle* ; and *Piers Plowman* (B-Text) xv. 321 *it ar þis pore freres*.

851-61 Chaucer's addition.

857 *Love is noght oold as whan that it is newe* : ' Love grown old is not like love when it is new '

859 *To dyen in the cas* : '⟨even⟩ in the event of death', i. e. even though my death may be the result ; cp. *for to be deed* 364.

872 *turne agayn* : ' return '.

880 *lyk a worm* : i. e. naked ; cp. ' nakid as a worme was she ', *Romaunt of the Rose* 454. The Oxford Dictionary quotes from *Gregory's Chronicle* : ' The Lorde Schalys . . . laye there dispoyly, nakyd as a worme ' ; and Skeat cites from the Coventry Mysteries ' I walke as werme, withoute wede '. All these are from the French *nu comme un ver*.
There is nothing in the Latin equivalent to ll. 880-3.

881 *Remembre yow* : note the reflexive dative, which was much commoner in Middle English than it is now : e. g. *wondred hem* 333, *yow avyse* 350, *conformynge hire* 546, *hasten hem* 978.

885 *As voucheth sauf* : imperative, ' deign '. See note to l. 7.

903 *a lyves creature*: 'a living creature'; cp. *Troilus* iv. 251 f.

> Acorsed be that day which that Natúre
> Shoop me to be a lives creatùre.

It springs from the Old English adverbial use of the genitive sg. *līfes*, meaning 'alive', e. g. *hē wæs līfes* 'he was alive'.

905 *Was evere in suspect*: 'always regarded with suspicion'; *have in suspect* is the commoner phrase.

911 *Agayns his doghter ... goth he*: 'he goes to meet his daughter'; the usual Middle English sense of *agayn(s)* with a verb of motion.

913 *as it myghte be*: 'as best he could'.

916 f. *For rude was the clooth, and moore of age*
> *By dayes fele, than at her mariàge*:

The Ellesmere and others of the best group of MSS., as well as MS. Harley 7334, have *and she moore of age*. This injures the metre; and the original, which says the cloth was *attrita senio*, is against it. Yet it shows intelligence, for if Griselda was married as early as was usual in old times, say at 12 like her daughter (l. 736), she would by now be about 25, and would be grown out of her old clothes. It is disquieting that the best MS. tradition should show traces of over-ingenious editing.

918–20 *Thus ... That*: 'In such wise ... that'.

924 *as by hire contenàunce*: 'to judge from her demeanour'.

925–31 Petrarch has only: *quippe cum in mediis opibus, inops semper spiritu vixisset atque humilis.*

927 *No tendre mouth, noon herte delicaat*: 'She cared not for the dainties of the table, nor was she luxury-loving at heart.' Of Nero the Monk says: He Rome brende *for his delicasie.* (*Monk's Tale* 489.)

932–8 This stanza is of Chaucer's invention.

934 *Namely of men*: 'particularly about men'. Perhaps the Clerk is here recalling the Wife of Bath's *Prologue* 688 ff., where she recounts the irritating ways of her fifth husband, Jankyn, 'who somtyme was a clerk of Oxenford':

> ... trusteth wel, it is an inpossible
> That any clerk wol spekè good of wyves ...
> By God! if wommen haddè writen stories,
> As clerkes han withinne hire oratories,
> They wolde han writen of men moore wikkednesse
> Than all the mark of Adam may redresse.

938 *but it be falle of-newe*: 'unless it has happened quite lately, too lately for me to know about it'. *of-newe* is the earlier form of *anew*.

947 *messáge*: probably 'messenger(s)' as in l. 738.

949-52 Petrarch has only: *devotissime venienti . . . ait.*

950 *swollen thoght*: 'feeling of injured pride'.

957-9 'And also that everybody, according to his rank, should be seated, served, and entertained as well as I can arrange it.'

965 *yvel biseye*: 'wretched looking'. *Besee* properly means 'to look at'; but the participle *beseen* (ME. *biseye*, &c.) is used in phrases like *wel biseye* 'seen to look well', 'goodly looking'; *richely biseye* 984, 'rich looking', &c.

966 *at the leestê weye*: 'at least', 'at any rate'; cp. *Man of Law's Prologue* 38:

> Thanne have ye doon youre devoir, attê leeste.

967 *Nat oonly, lord, that I am glad*: elliptical for 'Not only, lord, ⟨is it the case⟩ that I am glad'.

974-80 A fine piece of translation. The Latin is: *Et cum dicto, servilia mox instrumenta corripiens, domum verrere, mensas instruere, lectos sternere, hortarique alias coeperat, ancillae in modum fidelissimae.*

991-2 'And they would have children fairer and more acceptable (as rulers) because of her high birth.' Not in Petrarch.

995-1008: Chaucer's own comment, and claimed for him by the insertion of *Auctor* 'author' in the margin of the Ellesmere MS. Of the 'many-headed multitude' he held much the same opinion as Shakespeare; and a court poet by upbringing and interest, writing in the disturbed age that saw the Peasants' Revolt (1381), could hardly think otherwise. In the Envoy of his *Lak of Stedfastnesse*, addressed to the young King Richard II, he counsels forcible restoration of stability:

> Shew forth thy swerd of castigacioun,
> Dred God, do law, love trouthe and worthynesse,
> And *dryve* thy folk ageyn to stedfastnesse.

999 'Ever full of noisy chatter which has no value'; *clappyng* refers particularly to the clatter of a mill; cp. l. 1200 'Ay clappeth as a mille'; *jane* (from Old French *Gênes*, 'Genoa') was a Genoese silver coin of low value. *Mite*, the name of a Flemish copper coin, is used in the same phrase; e.g. *Troilus* iv. 684-6: And with hir tales, dere ynough a mite,

> Thise wommen . . . sette hem down.

1003 f. 'when the people everywhere stared ⟨raptly at the new marchioness⟩ because they were delighted for the mere novelty of having', &c.

1015 *dooth forth hire bisynesse*: 'goes on with her work'.

1021 *And koudê*: 'and knew how to do'.

1024 *to commende*: 'to praise' = *laudibus satiari*.

1026 'So well that nobody could have bettered her ⟨expressions⟩ of praise.'

1039 *as ye han doon mo*: 'as you have done to others'—a not uncommon use of *mo*: but she means 'one other'—herself. Latin: *unum bona fide te precor et moneo, ne hanc illis aculeis agites, quibus* alteram *agitasti*.

1047 *sad and constant as a wal*: because a wall is the type of stability. In the Towneley Miracle of *The Deluge*, l. 515, Noah says of the Dove:

> Thou art trew for to trist as ston in the wal.

1049 'This marquis inclined his heart to have compassion for', &c.

1066 *that oother, feithfully*: 'the second ⟨child⟩, assuredly'. The phrase *that oother* by wrong division gives *the tother*.

1070 f. A weak rendering of *quae divisim perdita videbantur, simul omnia recepisti*.

1086–1113 These five stanzas are Chaucer's addition, without hint from Petrarch or Boccaccio.

1088 I have retained the Ellesmere reading of this line, though it is exceptional. It seems to be one way out of the Corpus reading

> 'Grauntmercy lord God I thanke it ʒou', quod she,

which may represent a very early state of the text in which *God* stood above the line as a correction or variant for *lord* (or for *I*). Most MSS. have

> 'Grauntmercy lord, God thank it yow', quod she.

This is the other solution of the difficulty, and in its favour are the places cited in the note to l. 830.

1090 'Now I do not care if I die on this spot'; *right heere* is an example of a phrase once common that has passed out of English use, but survives in the United States; cp. *right theere* 374; *right tho* 544.

1092 *No fors of deeth*: 'what matters death?' cp. *Merchant's Tale* 591: It is no fors how longe that we pleye.

1098 *Hath doon yow kept*: 'has had you kept safe'. For the sense of *doon* cp. note to l. 253.

1100 *so sadly*: 'so firmly', 'so tight'.

1109 *And every wight hire joye and feeste maketh*: 'And everybody gives her a glad welcome and does her honour'; *feeste maken* from French *faire fête à* 'to do honour to'.

1120 *as hire oghte*: 'as was due to her', 'as was her right'.

For this quasi-impersonal use of *ought* with the dative pronoun, which is peculiar to Middle English, cp. *wel moore us oghte Receyven al in gree* 1150.

1137 f. 'And he was fortunate too in his marriage, *although he did not put his wife to any great test.*' It is Chaucer's way to give his subtlest wit the semblance of naivety. This is his answer to the Marquis's unconvincing apologia at ll. 1072–8; but it is besides a sly jest at the fallen estate of latter-day husbands.

1141 *this auctour* : Petrarch, who provides the groundwork for the next two stanzas.

1144 *For it were inportàble, though they wolde* : 'for it would be more than they could bear, even though they had the will.'

1148 *with heigh stile* : In the letter to Boccaccio embodying his translation, Petrarch writes : 'Hanc historiam *stylo* nunc *alio* retexere visum fuit . . .' 'I thought it worth while to tell this story again in *another style*', i. e. in Latin as contrasted with Boccaccio's version *vulgari stylo*, i. e. in Italian. Chaucer must have used a MS. that contained the bad reading *alto* for *alio* : and indeed *alto* is the reading of the marginal note in the Ellesmere MS. See Hendrickson, *Modern Philology* iv. 189 f.

1151 *sent* : 'sendeth'; contracted 3 sg. pres. indic.

1152 'For it is most reasonable that he should test what he created.'

1154 *As seith Seint Jame, if ye his pistel rede* : St. James i. 13–14 'Let no man say when he is tempted, I am tempted of God : for God cannot be tempted with evil, neither tempteth He any man : But every man is tempted, when he is drawn away of his own lust, and enticed.' Chaucer here gives *tempt* its modern sense, distinguishing temptation—the inducement to sin—from proving or testing, which is designed to purify.

1162 Here Petrarch's story ends, though he goes on to tell Boccaccio of the effect it had on two of his friends. One broke down twice in his reading for weeping; the other felt that it was too patently a fiction—too unreal; to which Petrarch replies with a ponderous list of classical examples of constancy.

1163 From here onwards all is Chaucer's own.

1168 *fair at eye* : 'fair at first sight': an earlier example of the idiom than those quoted in the Oxford Dictionary s.v. *Eye* § 4. It occurs also in *Knight's Tale* 2158.

This maystow understonde and seen at eye.

1169 'It would sooner break in two than bend.' Pliancy was an old test of good metal in a coin.

1170 *For the Wyves love of Bathe*: 'for the love of the Wife of Bath'. Note

(i) that Middle English uses the objective genitive freely, whereas Modern English, except in a few set phrases, uses *of*, reserving the inflexion for the subjective genitive, e.g. *the Wife of Bath's love of gaiety.*

(ii) The group genitive, with the *'s* at the end of the whole phrase to which it belongs, e.g. *the Wife of Bath's love*, is a comparatively modern construction. Chaucer always uses the type *The Clerkes Tale of Oxenford*, not 'the Clerk of Oxford's Tale'.

1171 *Whos lyf*: means no more than 'whom'. For a like use of *life* meaning 'person', see Gower, *Confessio Amantis* iv. 3043:

> *he ful ofte entriketh*
> *The lif which slepe schal be nyhte*

'He often deceives a sleeping man'.

1184 *youre tongè naille*: 'make fast your tonge as with nails', i.e. prevent it 'clapping like a mill' l. 1200.

1185 *Ne lat no clerk have cause or diligence*: *diligence* seems to be used to make the rime, perhaps in the strained sense 'opportunity for industry'.

1188 *Chichivache*, 'lean cow' (but really a corruption of *chichefac(h)e* 'lean face') is one of the creations of the early French school of railers against women. *Chichivache* was a monster whose sole diet was patient wives—hence its leanness. An early French poet, who saw the monster, says: 'She was ugly of face and body, and was called the "Chincheface". She had long teeth like hooks, and I assure you her eyes were as big as baskets and blazed as bright as torches; and she was quite six feet high.'

1190 *answereth at the countretaille*: 'answer back'. In order to check a tally or score, the person scored against kept a counter-tally. Hence, perhaps, Chaucer's sense: 'contest every attempt to score against you'.

1199 'Be fierce as is a tiger afar off in India'; but *tygre yond in Ynde* trapped Spenser, who thought *yond* must be an adjective 'ferocious'; and so writes in the *Faerie Queen* III. vii. 26:

> Nor halfe so fast ...
> Fled fearfull Daphne on th' Aegaean strond
> As Florimell fled from that monster *yond*.

See the editor's note in the Oxford Dictionary (*N.E.D.*).

1206 *couche as doth a quaille*: 'cower (or lie close) as a quail does' when hunted. The simile is found elsewhere, e.g. *Pearl* 1085, I stod as stylle as dased quayle.

1211 *as light as leef on lynde*: a proverbial alliterative

phrase, arising from the quick, light movements of leaves when the wind blows. The *lynde* or *lime* was chosen partly for the alliteration, partly because its wood was proverbially light. Cp. Poems of MS. Harley 2253 ed. Böddeker (1878) p. 166:

> In May hit murgeth when it dawes . . .
> Ant lef is lyht on lynde.

Bihoolde the murye wordes of the Hoost, &c. These lines are found in the Ellesmere and other good MSS. If genuine, they are a cancelled part of a link, originally designed to join *The Clerkes Tale* to the tale next following, but abandoned when the device of echoing the Clerk's last words in the first line of the *Merchant's Prologue* was hit upon, and in part incorporated into the link following Chaucer's own tale of *Melibeus*:

> Whan ended was my tale of Melibee,
> And of Prudénce and hire benignytee,
> Oure Hostè seyde, 'As I am feithful man,
> And by that precious corpus Madrian,
> I haddè levere than a barel ale
> That goodè lief my wyf hadde herd this tale!
> For she nys nothyng of swich paciènce
> As was this Melibeus wyf Prudénce.
> By Goddes bones! &c.

Against their genuineness it might be argued that they were hatched up by an early editor who had the *Melibeus* link before him, and eked it out with tags from elsewhere. But they have a Chaucerian ring, and as they occur in MSS. like Ellesmere, which have the correct junction with the *Merchant's Tale*, and so needed no newly-forged link, they are probably Chaucer's rough draft, accidentally preserved.

[7] Cp. *Dethe of Blaunche* 42:

> But thyng that wol nat be, lat it be stille.

Merchant's Prologue

1213 *Wepyng and waylyng*: note how the Merchant picks up the last words of *The Clerkes Tale*.

1221 *What sholde I?* 'Why should I?'

1222 *at al*: 'altogether', 'through and through'.

1226 *unbounden*: 'freed from the bonds of marriage'.

1230 *seint Thomas of Ynde*: the apostle Thomas, whose missionary labours in India are mentioned by St. Jerome. He was buried in Madras.

1231-2: Chaucer is seldom sweeping in his statements. He loves a reservation.

CHAUCER'S ENGLISH

§ 1. **Changes of Meaning.**—In *The Clerkes Tale* Chaucer uses few words that have no recognizable descendants in modern English; and some of these, like *wrye* 887 (which is glossed by *covere* in the Ellesmere MS.), must have been going out of use already in the fifteenth century. But if we try to assign a precise meaning to each word and phrase, it appears at once that he uses many words in senses no longer common. That Griselda, bereft of her children, should be *sad* (693) seems natural enough; yet it puzzled her husband—because Chaucer uses *sad* to mean not 'sorrowful', but 'steadfast', 'unmoved'. *Bounty*, as an abstract, now means one particular form of goodness—'liberal giving'; but in ll. 157, 159, &c., it means 'goodness' generally. Such marked divergencies are not likely to escape attention.

But many words have changed more subtly. It is easy to pass over 'It woldè *rather* breste a-two than plye' 1169 without noticing that *rather* has here the temporal sense 'sooner', which is now obsolete. When we say 'she looked pale' we take up the observer's standpoint, and *looked* is virtually a passive, meaning 'was seen to be': but in *she looked with ful palè face* 340, the old active meaning still lingers. We can use *nurture* to cover the whole upbringing of a child, but not *nourish*, as Chaucer does at l. 399, or *feed* 397, or *foster* 1043. Again, a modern poet would hardly be flattered if his *rhetoric* were praised, for the word has come to connote artificiality rather than art: and the collocation of *rhetoric* and *sweet* (l. 32) would be scarcely possible nowadays, when *rhetoric* suggests a dignified aloofness, and *sweet* has lost too much in dignity to be paired with it. The Glossary provides many other examples.

§ 2. **Dialect.**—Chaucer wrote in the dialect of London, which by his time was just attaining to supremacy as the literary language of England. Hence his language is much easier to us than that of contemporary works in other dialects, such as *Sir Gawayne* or *Piers Plowman*.

Note: His rimes, always instructive, occasionally show one distinctive feature of the Kentish dialect. An Anglo-Saxon etymological *y* became *i* always in Northern Middle English, and commonly in the Midlands; in the western districts of the South and Midlands it often appears as *u*; in Kentish it became *e*. *The Clerkes Tale* happens to

Language

exhibit all these developments in two words :—OE. *lystan* v. yields *list* 647, *lust* 322, and *lest(e)* 105 (riming with *requeste*); OE. *myrge* adj. yields *myrie* 9, *murie* 15, *merie* 615 (riming with *herye*, OE. *herian*), and here, quite exceptionally, modern English has standardized the Kentish form *merry* instead of normal East Midland *mirry*. So at ll. 897–9 *weye* (OE. *weg-*) rimes with *dreye* (OE. *drȳge*) ' dry '; at ll. 972–3, *stente* (OE. *styntan*) rimes with *entente*; at ll. 1056–7 *kesse* (OE. *cyssan*) rimes with *stedfastnesse*; and such rimes are exact only in South-Eastern districts.

§ 3. **Spelling and Pronunciation.**—The spelling of a good MS. like the Ellesmere is fairly regular; and it is roughly phonetic in the sense that every letter in the spelling represents a sound. But it is a mistake to suppose that an initiated person can tell exactly how Chaucer pronounced each sound. There are many matters of doubt ; and, after all, we read Shakespeare and later writers very well without considering over-nicely the details of pronunciation in their time.

(i) SYLLABLES.—Words have been shortened since Chaucer's day. Thus the rimes in ll. 449–53 are not identical, because *thro/we*, *kno/we* have each two syllables. And the verse will seem halting unless inflexional *-es*, *-ed*, as in *spous/ed* 3, *ned/es* 11 are pronounced as separate syllables (with some exceptions in longer words). For syllabic final *-e* see § 4.

(ii) CONSONANTS.—There are no silent consonant symbols :— Initial *k* in *kn-* was still pronounced, so that *knyghtes* and *nyghtes* are distinct : and in like manner *wrynge* is distinguished from *rynge(s)*. *Light* (OE. *līht*) cannot rime with *lite* (OE. *lȳt*) ' little ', because *gh*, though it was weakening, retained something of the sound heard in Scotch *loch*. *r* is always slightly trilled, e. g. initially and finally in *rather*, medially in *worthy*.

(iii) VOWELS.—For the vowels the best rough rule is to follow the Continental pronunciation of Latin, bearing in mind that *i* and *y* represent the same vowel sounds.

(*a*) Short *a, e, i, o, u* are pronounced respectively as in French *patte*, English *pet, pit, pot, put*.

Note : Short *u* is regularly spelt *o* when it occurs alongside *m, n, i,* which, in their script forms, are easily confused with *u* (see the facsimile plate) :—e. g. *tonge* (OE. *tunge*) ; *som* (OE. *sum*) ; *come* (OE. *cuman*) ; *love* (OE. *lufu*) ; *sone* (OE. *sunu*) ' son ' ; *woned* (OE. *(ge)-wunad*) 339, &c.

(*b*) Long *ā, ī, ū* are pronounced respectively as in *father, police, rude*. Long *ē* and *ō* have both open and close sounds, which are usually distinguished in the rimes. Close *ẹ̄* is pronounced as in French *été* ; open *ę̄* as in English ' air ' ; close *ọ̄* as

65   F 2

in French 'eau'; open ϱ as in English 'oar'. The distinction
of the open and close sounds in Chaucer is often difficult.

Note : Long *ū* is always spelt *ou* (*ow*), e.g. *sours, mouth*, &c.

Long *ē*, *ō* are often spelt *ee*, *oo*, e.g. *heere* adv., *hooste*; *ā* is sometimes doubled, e.g. *glaade* 822.

Long close *ę̄* is sometimes distinguished by the spelling *ie*, e.g. *lie*ʒ
479; *chiere* 238, 241 (beside *cheere* 7). The modern spelling *ea* usually
indicates that the word had open *ę̄* in Chaucer's time, e.g. in *meat, feat*
compared with *meet, feet* which had close *ę̄*. Words which have *oo* in
modern spelling, e.g. *roat, foot*, had close *ǭ* in Chaucer's day.

(iv) ACCENTUATION.—In English words the stress accent
falls practically as in modern English. But French words
borrowed into English were in a transitional stage. In French
the last stem syllable of nouns is stressed rather more than the
others. In English nouns the first syllable carries a very strong
stress, and the later syllables are relatively weak. Ultimately
most borrowings from French followed the English system :
but in Chaucer they more often retain their original accentuation, e.g. *colóur, coráge*. In polysyllables like *áventúre, óbeisánce*
it is hard to say whether the first or the last accented syllable
bears the greater stress. Unusual accentuation is indicated
throughout the text : see p. xxv.

§ 4. **Inflexions. Final -e.**—In some ways the inflexions in
Chaucer are very like those of early modern English as it is
recorded in the Authorized Version of 1611. But whereas
in the following two or three centuries final *-e* is added almost
at random by scribes and printers, in Chaucer's English it
usually has a grammatical value, and it is commonly pronounced as a distinct syllable. It represents an Old English
unaccented vowel, whether final (as *-a, -e, -o, -u*) or followed in
OE. by flexional *-n*, *-m* (as *-an, -en, -on, -um*) ; and it also represents Old French final *-e*.

Its commonest occurrences in inflexion are :—

(i) In the plural of all adjectives (except polysyllables), e.g.
oldė synnes 13.

(ii) In the singular of weak adjectives (see § 6 below), e.g.
Hir meekė preyere 141.

(iii) In various verbal inflexions, particularly

    (*a*) in the infinitive, e.g. *to chesė* 153.

    (*b*) in the plural of the present indicative, e.g. *knowė* 528, 622.

    (*c*) in the weak pa. t. sg. & pl., e.g. *taughtė* 40, *wentė* 86.

    (*d*) in the pres. and pa. subj. sgs., e.g. *as hym lestė* 161.

    (*e*) in the strong past participle, e.g. *borė* 401.

N.B. In (*a*), (*b*), (*e*), and in the plurals under (*c*), *-en* is found as well as *-e*. Generally *-en* is used before a word beginning with a vowel or *h*, and *-e* before a word beginning with a consonant.

(iv) As the ending of many adverbs, e.g. *newè* 3, *fastè* 978.

From failure to recognize the possible syllabic value of final *-e* arose the belief, which so great a critic as Dryden shared, that Chaucer's rhythms are crude and rough; and their music was not recovered until Tyrwhitt published his edition (1775–8).

§ 5. **Nouns.**—The regular endings are :—

	Singular.	Plural.
Nom. Acc.	—	*-es.*
Gen.	*-es.*	*-es.*
Dat.	*-(e).*	*-es.*

Note : (*a*) *-es* is a separate syllable, except in words of three or more syllables, where *-e* may be silent; for instance :—*felawes* 282.

(*b*) Some nouns from French, of which the singular ends in *t*, add *z* direct in the plural, e. g. *juggementz* 439, *subgetz* 482.

(*c*) *-e* often appears in spelling as the ending of the dative singular, but it is seldom established by the rhythm.

(*d*) Survivals from Old English are :—

(i) The uninflected gen. sg. of nouns in *-er* expressing relation-ship : *doghter name* 608, *fader hous* 896 (beside *fadres hous* 809).
(ii) The uninflected plural of neuter nouns with long stems : *twelf yeer* 736. (iii) One plural in *-en* : *eyen* (OE. *ēagan*) 669.

§ 6. **Adjectives.**—The adjective, which was to lose all trace of inflexion in the course of the fifteenth century, is still inflected in Chaucer :—The plural of all adjectives ends in *-e* : *oure oldè synnes* 13 ; *swichè gestes* 339. The singular of all adjectives ends in *-e* when they follow the weak declension, e. g. *Hir meekè preyere* 141, *this yongè mayden* 210, *O goodè God* 852.

Note : (*a*) The weak form of an adjective is used chiefly after the demonstratives *the*, *this*, *her*, &c.; in the vocative ; and before proper names, among which is to be reckoned *God* (e. g. *hyè God* 206).

(*b*) Polysyllabic adjectives usually have no inflexion.

§ 7. **Pronouns.**
(i) 3rd PERSON.—The personal pronoun of the third person is, in the plural: Nom. *they*, Poss. *hir(e)*, Obj. *hem*. Thus of the three forms that English borrowed from Norse (*they*, *their*, *them*), only the first had been accepted in the London dialect up to the end of the fourteenth century.

Note : (*a*). The possessive plural *hir(e)* 'their' is in form the same as the poss. sing. fem. *hir(e)* 'her'; see 227 n., 380 n.

(*b*). The possessive of *it* is *his*, e. g. in ll. 49, 50, 618.

(*c*). The old indefinite pronoun *man*, later *men*, 'one', seems to be preserved in *men clepeth* 'one calls' 115, though most MSS. have *men clepe(n)*, with plural verb.

(ii) 2nd PERSON.—The singular pronouns *thou, thee* are still freely used in familiar talk, or when a superior addresses an inferior. The polite plurals *ye, you* are preferred in formal language, and when a person addresses his equal or superior. *You* obj. is never confused with *ye* nom.

(iii) RELATIVE.—**That** is the usual relative, e. g. *this worthy man,* That *taughtĕ me this tale* 40; *to thee,* that *born art of a smal villáge* 483.

Which (usually preceded by *the* or followed by *that*) is also common, e. g. *a man* Which that *was holden povrest of hem alle* 205; *the village, of* the which *I tolde* 272; *Lordes and ladyes . . . The* whiche that *to the feestĕ weren y-prayed* 269. Combination with *as* is rarer, e. g. *Hir tretys,* which as *ye shal after heere* 331.

Who nom. is only interrogative or indefinite; but the oblique cases *whos, whom* (sometimes combined with *that*), are occasionally used as relatives; e. g. *this clerk,* whos *re-thorikĕ* 32; *his lust . . . To* whom that *she was yeven* 758.

§ 8. Verbs.—(i) THE PRESENT INDICATIVE.

Singular.	Plural.
(*i*)*ch com-e*	*we com-e*(*n*)
thou com-(*e*)*st*	*ye com-e*(*n*)
he com-(*e*)*th*	*they com-e*(*n*)

Note: (*a*) The plural -*e*(*n*) is the typical inflexion of the Midland dialect (Southern dialects have (*e*)*th,* Northern (*e*)*s*).

(*b*) The 3rd pers. sing. ends in (*e*)*th,* not -(*e*)*s.* The Northern ending -(*e*)*s* did not become usual in London until Elizabethan times.

(*c*) When the stem ends in *d* or *t,* the 3rd pers. sing. is sometimes contracted:—*smyt* 122 n., *last* 266, *lust* 322, *sit* 460, *sent* 1151 = *smyteth, lasteth,* &c.

(ii) THE IMPERATIVE PLURAL, which is used politely where a single person is addressed, ends in (*e*)*th* or -*e*:—in ll. 7–19 we have *beth . . . telle . . . precheth . . . telle . . . keepe . . . speketh.*

(iii) THE PAST PARTICIPLE often retains its old prefix *y-* (OE. *ge-*), which is lost very early in Northern dialects. In strong verbs it ends in -(*e*)*n* or -*e,* whereas modern English (like the Northern dialect of Middle English) has regularly -*n.* So Chaucer has four types:—*y-bore* 310, 443; *y-born* 72; *born* 444; *bore* 401.

The remaining inflexions of the verb present little difficulty, and their subsequent history is comprised in the loss of inflexional -*e,* -*en*; the loss of distinctive forms of the 2nd person singular; and the loss of the subjunctive.

NOTE ON THE METRE

Rimes apart, the basis of all three metres used in the text is a line of five stresses ; and if stressed syllables be represented by $\angle$ and unstressed by ×, the norm is

$$\times \; \angle \; | \; \times \; \angle \; | \; \times \; \angle \; | \; \times \; \angle \; | \; \times \; ' \; | \; (\times)$$

Sir Clérk | of Óx|enfórd | oure Hóost|è séyd|è

That final -*e* at the line ending makes a 'feminine' rime is shown by such couplets as

> That streight was comen fro the court of *Romè*:
> Ful loude he soong ' Com hider, lovè, *to me* '.　　　*Gen. Prol* 672.

There is a light and mobile caesura that usually falls after the second or third foot ; and variety and fluency are increased by the skilful running over of the sense from one line to the next, e.g. ll. 122 ff.

> And deeth manaceth every age, and smyt
> In ech estaat, for ther escapeth noon ;
> And also certein as we knowe echoon
> That we shul deye, as uncerteyn we alle
> Been of that day whan deeth shal on us falle.

Besides, Chaucer avoids monotony by the same devices of inverted stress, and substitution of light for heavy stresses, that are usual in Shakespeare, e.g.

Kéepe hem | in stóor | til so | be that | y'endít|è.

And one variation in which the first foot is a single stressed syllable is a common stumbling-block, e. g.

Twén|ty bóok|es clád | in blák | or réed.　　　*Gen. Prol.* 294.

Elision of final -*e* which would normally be syllabic is usual before a word beginning with a vowel or *h*, e. g. *y'endite* 17 ; *th'erthè* 203 ; *to/ Janic/l' of which/* 404 ; and

Ye rýdę | as cóy | and stíllę | as dóoth | a máydè 2.

Words like *evere, nevere, povere, owene,* are treated as *evre, nevre, povre, owne* ; i.e. they are disyllabic before words beginning with a consonant, e. g.

myn ówn/è pép/lè déer/è 143 ; *this póv/rè cré/atúr/è* 232.

and monosyllabic before a vowel or *h*, e. g.

I név/r' erst thóught/è 144 ; *youre póv/r' arráy* 467.

Practice in reading gives better results than elaborate metrical analysis, for there is no one way of reading English metres that suits all ears.

GLOSSARY

This Glossary aims at recording forms and meanings that might trouble a reader accustomed to modern English. Not all the words in the text are included, nor all the references to those selected for explanation. But the space saved has been employed to give a very full list of words (still familiar enough and easily recognizable) which Chaucer used with a shade of meaning that is no longer common: for they are a main cause of misunderstanding, or of imperfect understanding.

The order is strictly alphabetical. References marked with an asterisk do not belong to *The Clerkes Tale*.

abaysed, abayst, *pp. adj.* abashed, 317, 1011, 1108.

abreyde, *pa. t.* came to (herself), 1061.

abyde, *v.* to wait for, 119; wait on, endure, 757; remain, 1106.

accident, *sb.* change from normal, 607.

acquite (*hym*), *v.* acquit (himself), 936.

affraye, *v.* to frighten, 455.

after, *conj.* according as, 203. *prep.* according to, 327, 504, 785, 962.

agayn, ageyn, *prep.* against, 170. *adv.* back again, 567, 575, 808, 872 n., 884; *caught agayn* recovered, 1110.

agayns, *prep.* : *go agayns* to go to meet, 911 n.

agon *pp.* gone; dead, 632.

al, *conj.* although, 99, 1138.

allyes, *sb pl.* alloys, 1167.

algate, *adv.* in every way, 855.

amblyng, *pres. p adj.* : *wel amblyng* easy-paced, suited to a lady, 388.

ameve, *v.* to be disturbed, 498.

among, *prep.* : *among al this* meanwhile, 785.

a-morwe, *adv.* in the morning, 1214.

anon, *adv.* at once, forthwith, 290, 772; for a while, 435; *see* 602 n.

äornement, *sb.* ornament, 258.

apayed, *pp. adj.* pleased; *yvele apayed* ill at ease, troubled, 1052.

apérceyve, *v.* to perceive, 600.

arace, *v.* to tear away, remove, 1103.

archiwyves, *sb. pl.* masterly wives, 1195.

array, *sb.* order, 262; equipment, apparel, 273, 383, 467; pomp, 275; plight, 670.

arraye, *v.* to arrange, 961.

art, *sb.* branch of learning, 35.

as, *adv.* and *conj.* as if, 168, 513. *See* 7 n., 48 n.

assay, *sb.* trial, 1166; *tempted in assay* put to the test, 621.

astoned, astonyed, *pa. t.* and *pp.* struck with amazement, 316, 337.

asúre, *sb.* azure, blue, 254.

aswowne, *adj.* in a swoon, 1079.

at-on, *adv.* at one; *bringen at-on* to reconcile, 437 [*cp.* atone].

atte = *at the*, 749, &c.

a-two, *adv.* in two, 1169.

auctour, *sb.* author, 1141.

audience, *sb.* hearing, 637.

áventàille, *sb.* the movable front of a helmet, which could be raised to permit free breathing; *hence* the spot for a vital thrust in a contest, 1204.

áventùre, *sb.* (strange) happening, 15; chance, 812; *par áventùre* perchance, 234.

avyse, (*upon*), *v. reflex.* to think (over), consider, 238; (implying ultimate refusal), 350.

axe, *v.* to ask, demand, 25, 326.

70

ayeyns, *prep.* against, contrary to, 320. *See* agayns.

bachelrye, *sb.* young knights, 270.
bar, *pa. t.* (of *bere*) bore ; *bar so soore* took so hardly, 85.
barm, *sb.* bosom, 551.
beede, *v.* to offer, 360.
beny(n)gne, *adj.* gentle, modest, 343, &c.
bidaffed, *pp.* fooled, 1191.
bigile, *v.* to beguile, 252.
biseke, *v.* to beseech, 178, 592.
biseye, *pp.* in *yvel biseye*, wretched looking, 965 n., 984.
biside, *adv.* round about, 416.
bisy, *adj.* active, 134 n.
bisynesse, *sb.* : *to doon hire bisynesse* to do her best, 592. *See* 195 n.
bitake, *v.* to commit (to the care of), 161, 559.
bityde, *v.* (*with dat.*) happen (to), 79.
blesse, blisse, *v.* to mark with the sign of the Cross, 553, 679.
boistously, *adv.* roughly, loudly, 791.
bord, *sb.* table (= wedding-breakfast) 3.
bo(u)ntee, *sb.* goodness, 157, 159.
breste, *v.* to break, 1169.
bulle, *sb.* a papal bull, 739.
but, *conj.* unless, 570 ; otherwise than, 602, 721.
buxomly, *adv.* submissively, 186.

caas, cas, *sb.* happening, 316 ; occasion, 430 ; case, emergency, plight, 488, 561.
camáille, *sb.* camel, 1196.
cesse (*of*), *v.* to cease, desist (from), 154.
chace, *v.* to pursue (a story), 341.
chamberere, *sb.* chambermaid, 819.
charge, *sb.* weight (of responsibility), 163 ; duties, 193.
charitee, *sb.* loving kindness, 221.
chese, *v.* to choose, 130, 153.
cheste, *sb.* coffin, 29.
chesynge, *sb.* (the) choice, 162 n.
chichivache, *sb.* a monster, 1188 n.
chiere, che(e)re, *sb.* face, appearance,

141, 238, 241 ; demeanour, 576 ; frame of mind, 7, 298 ; gladness, 1112 ; *cheere make* to assume (*or* wear) an expression, 535, 678.
choys, *sb.* choice, 154.
circumstances, *sb. pl.* attentions, 584 n.
clappe, *v.* to clatter, talk noisily, 1200.
clappynge, *sb.* noisy chatter, 999.
cleere, *adj.* shining bright, 779.
clene, *adj.*, pure, 836.
clepe, *v.* to call, name, 115.
collacioun, *sb.* conference, 325.
colóurs, *sb. pl.* rhetorical embellishments, 16.
commune, *sb. collective*, commons, people below the rank of lord, 70. *adj.* common, of the community, 431.
compleyne, *v.* to lament, 530.
condicioun, *sb.* nature, 701.
contenaunce, *sb.* demeanour, 708.
continuynge, *pres. p.* maintaining, 1048.
convoyen, *v.* to introduce, 55 ; to conduct, 391.
coráge, *sb.* heart, 511 ; mind, thoughts, 220 ; desire, 907.
costage, *sb.* costliness, richness, 1126.
cote, *sb.* (peasant's) cottage, 398.
couche, *v.* to cower, 1206 n.
countretaille, *sb.* counter-tally, 1190 n.
courtepy, *sb.* a short cloak of coarse stuff, *Prol.* 290*.
coy, *adj.* silent from modesty, 2 n.
crien, *v.* to beseech, 801.
croys, *sb.* cross, 556.
cure, *sb.* occupation, responsibility, 82 ; attention, *Prol.* 303* [not connected with *care*].
cursednesse, *sb.* crabbedness, 1239*.

deed, *adj.* dead, 29.
deface, *v.* blot out, efface, 510.
delicaat, *adj.* lovely, 682 ; perverted by luxury, 927 n.
delit, *sb.* joy, delight, 68.
délitàble, *adj.* delectable, 62, 199.
demand, *sb.* question, 348.
departe, *v.* to separate ; wean, 618.
despitously, *adv.* pitilessly, 535.

devoir, *sb.* duty, office, 966.

devyse, *v.* to describe, 52 ; to conceive of, 675.

deyntee, *sb.* a joy, 1112.

deyntevous, *adj.* choice ; rich, 265.

diffame, *sb.* ill-fame, 540, 730.

dighte, *v.* to put in order, 974.

digne, *adj.* worthy, 411, 818.

diligence, *sb.* attention, 230 ; *dooth al his diligence* gives all his care, 195 n.

discryve, *v.* to describe, 43.

dishonèste, *adj.* dishonourable, causing dishonour, 876.

dísparàge, *sb.* disparagement, 908.

dispence, *sb.* expenditure, 1209.

dispende, *v.* to spend, 1123.

dispoillen, *v.* to strip (of clothes), undress, 374.

doom, *sb.* judgement, 1000.

doon, *v.* to do, act, 493 ; to cause, 353 ; *doon make* to have (a thing) made, 253 n.; cp. 863 ; 1098.

dowáire, dowere, *sb.* dowry, 807, 848.

drad, *pp.* dreaded, held in awe, 69. *pa. t.* **dredde**, 181.

drede, *sb.* fear, doubt, 838 n., 865.

dresse (*me*), *v.* to address (myself), to direct (my) attention, 1007 ; to incline, 1049 n.

dreye, *adj.*, dry, 899 [Kentish form].

dure, *v.* to last, endure, 166, 825.

dwellen, *v.* to tarry ; to dwell ; 36.

echoon, *pron.* each (one), 124.

eek, *adv.* besides, also, 83.

egre, *adj.* fierce and keen, 1199.

eldres, *sb. pl.* ancestors, 65.

elles, *adv.* else ; *or elles that . . . or elles* either because . . . or because, 90.

encresse, *v.* to increase, 50.

enlumyne (*of*), *v.* illuminate (with), 33 n.

entente, *sb.* meaning, purpose, thought, 127, 186, 189.

entraille, *sb.* maw, 1188.

ernestful, *adj.* serious, 1175.

erst, *adv.* before, 144 ; *thanne at erst* then for the first time, 985.

ese, *sb.* comfort, 664.

esily, *adv.* without troubles, 423.

estaat, *sb.* rank, condition of life, 123 ; condition of affairs, 610.

evene, *adj.* composed, 811.

execucioun, *sb.* : *doon execucioun on*, execute, carry out, 522.

fader, *sb.* father ; *fadres oldè*, distant ancestors, 61.

falle, *v.* to appertain, 259. *See* fil.

fare, *v.* to go, 1217* ; *pp.* 896.

fayn, *adv.* fain, gladly, 696.

feeste (*maken*), to welcome, 1109 n.

feet, *sb.* practice, 429.

feithfully, *adv.* assuredly, 1066 ; wholeheartedly, 1111.

felawe, *sb.* companion, 282.

fele, *adj.* many, 917.

fer, *adv.* far, 25.

ferde, *pa. t.* (of *fare*)behaved, 1060.

fette, *pa. t.* (of *fecchen*) fetched, 301.

fey, *sb.* faith, 9.

feyntyng, *sb.* slackening in endeavour, failing, 970.

figúres, *sb. pl.* figures of speech proper to poetic diction : hyperbole, metaphor, and the like, 16.

fil, *pa. t.* (of *falle*) happened, 235, 449 ; **falle**, *pp.* 938.

fithele, *sb.* fiddle, *Prol.* 296*.

flokmeele, *adv.* in flocks, in crowds, 86 [*cp.* piece-meal].

folwe, *v.* to imitate, 1189.

fonde, *v.* to try, 283.

for, *conj.* because, 216, 724. *prep.* because of, 607.

forgoon, *v.* to forgo, give up, 171.

fors, *sb.* force : *no fors* (*of*) what matter ? 1092 n.

forth, *adv.* : *forth to tellen* to tell on 39 ; *dooth forth hire bisynesse* goes on doing her work, 1015.

forther, *adj.* more advanced, 712.

foryelde, *v.* to repay, to requite, 831.

foryetful, *adj.* forgetful, 472.

foryeve, *v.* to forgive, 526.

fostre, *v.* to foster; to feed and tend, 222; to bring up, 593, 834.

foul, *adj.* ugly, 1209.

fowel, *sb.* bird (of prey), 683.

freletee, *sb.* frailty, liability to sin, 1160.

frere, *sb.* friar, 12.

ful, *adv. intensive,* 187, &c.

game, *sb.* sport; *neuere . . in ernest ne in game* never on any occasion, 609 n.

gan, *pa. t. sg.,* **gonne,** *pl.* 1103 (*used with infin. to form a simple past tense*); 289 n.

geere, *sb.* clothing, 372.

gentil, *adj.* noble, 72, 131; *sb.* a noble, 480.

gentillesse, *sb.* nobility; what befits one of high birth, 593.

gerdoun, *sb.* guerdon, recompense, 883.

gla(a)de, *v. trans.* to cheer, 1107; 822 n.

gonne, *see* gan.

goost, *sb.* spirit, 926.

governaille, *sb.* control, management (of the household), 1192.

governaunce, *sb.* dispositions, 994.

grauntmercy, *interj.* thanks! 1088 [OFr. *grand merci* = great reward (may you have)].

grave, *v.* to bury, 681.

gree, *sb.* goodwill; *in gree* gladly, without murmuring, 1151.

grette, *pa. t.* greeted, saluted, 952.

greve, *v.* to vex, 889.

grucche, *v. intrans.* grumble, murmur, 170. *trans.* to resent, 354.

gyde, *v.* to conduct, guide, 776.

gye, *v.* to guide, govern, 75.

habundant (*of*), *adj.* abounding (in); *h. of vitáille* productive, rich, 59.

han, *pl. pres. indic.* have, 23.

hardily, *adv.* assuredly, 25.

hardinesse, *sb.* boldness, 93.

heeres, heris, *sb. pl.* hair, 379, 1085.

heest(e), *sb.* hest, command, 128, 529.

heigh, hy, *adj.* high, 18, 45; supreme, 418.

hente, *v.* to get hold of, *Prol.* 299*; *pa. t.* snatched, took, 534; *pp.* 676.

herbergage, *sb. collect.* dwellings, 201.

hertely, *adj.* proceeding from the heart, sincere, 176, 502.

herye, *v.* to praise, 616.

hevynesse, *sb.* sorrow, 95, 432.

highte, *v. passive* was called, 32, 63, &c. *active pa. t.* promised, 496.

holde, *v.* to maintain, 1189; to take *or* keep to (a road), 287; *pp.* holde(n), 273; regarded as, 205.

honéste, *adj.* honourable, 333.

honéstetee, *sb.* honour, 422 n.

hool, *adj.* whole, full; *in hool entente* whole-heartedly, 861.

humanitee, *sb.* graciousness, 92.

impertinent, *adj.* not to the point, 54.

inportàble, *adj.* impossible to bear, 1144 n.

inwith, *prep.* within, 870

jane, *sb.* a small Genoese coin, 999 n.

keepe, *sb.* heed, 1058.

kembd, *pp.* combed, 379 [*cp.* unkempt].

kepte, *pa. t.* (of *kepe*) watched over, 223.

kesse, *v.* kiss, 1057 [Kentish form].

knave-child, *sb.* boy, 444.

konnyngly, *adv.* expertly, 1017.

koude, *pa. t.* could, knew how to (do), 90, 1021 n. [*l* in *could* first appears in the 16th century.]

kouth, *pp.* known, 942.

lappe, *sb.* piece of cloth (to serve as a wrapping), 585.

last, *pres. indic. 3 sg.* extends, 266 n.

lauriat, *adj.* laurel-crowned, 31 n.

leese, *v.* to lose, 508; *pp.* lorn, 1071.

leet, *pa. t. 3 sg.* to let, allow, 82.

leeve (*on*), *v.* believe (in), trust, 1001.

legende, *sb.* an instructive story, [4].

lenger, *adj. compar.* longer, 300, 687.

lest, *sb.* desire, 619 [Kentish form].

leste, liste, *subjunctive*; **list,** *indic.*: *impers. with dat.* it please(s), 105 n., 111, 647. *See* lust. [*leste* is Kentish.]

lete, *v.* to leave, abandon, 745.

lette, *sb.* delay, 300.

lette, *v.* to delay, 389.

levere, *adj.* and *adv.* rather, 444 n., [3].

lief, *adj.* beloved, 479.

lige, *sb.* one who owes allegiance, vassal, 67; **lige-man,** 310.

like, *v. with dat.* to please, 506; *impers.* it pleases, 106 n., 311.

likerous, *adj.* luxurious; *likerous lust,* desire of luxury, 214.

liklihede, liklynesse, *sb.* probability; *by l.* in accordance with probability, 396, 448.

lite, *sb.* little, 935.

longe, *v.* to belong; *the labour which that longeth unto me* = my work, 285.

lookyng, *sb.* expression (of the face), 514.

loore, *sb.* wisdom, 87; knowledge, 788.

lorn, *pp.* lost, 1071. *See* leese.

lust, *v. impers. 3 sg.* (= *lusteth*) it pleases, 322. *See* leste.

lust, *sb.* pleasure (*with no bad sense*), 80, 352.

lusty, *adj.* pleasant, rich, 59.

lynd(e), *sb.* linden *or* lime-tree; *sometimes, by extension,* any tree, 1211 n.

lyves, *adv.* alive, 903 n.

maistrie, *sb.* ascendancy, sway, 1172.

make, *sb.* mate, 840.

manáce, *v.* to menace, threaten, 122.

maner, manére, *sb.* way, manner, 174; kind : *a maner sergeant,* 519 n.

maydenhede, *sb.* maidenhood, 837.

maystow = *mayst thou,* 265.

mazednesse, *sb.* amazement, stupor, 1061.

meede, *sb.* meed; *to my meede* as my recompense, 885.

meeste, *adj. superl.* greatest, 131.

men, *pron. indef.* one, 115. [Note the singular verb.]

message, *sb.* messengers, 738 n., 947.

mesúre, *sb.* moderation, 622.

mete, *sb.* food (in general), 1028.

mo, *adj.* more (in number), other, 318, 449; others, 1039 n.

moot(e), *v.* may, 557; must, 11; **moste,** *pa. t.* might, 550.

mowe, *v.* may, 529.

muchel, *adj.* much, 1238*, 1241*.

murie, *see* myrie.

murmur(e), *sb.* outcry, complaint, 628, 635; rumour, 726.

myrie, *adj.* merry, 9; **murie,** 15; **merye,** 615.

naille, *v.* to make fast, 1184 n.

namely, *adv.* especially, 484, &c.

nas = *ne was* was not, *Prol.* 4*.

nat, *negative* not, 12, &c.

nathele(e)s, *adv.* none the less, nevertheless, 148, 733.

nay, *sb.* denial; *it is no nay* there is no denying it, 817.

nempne, *v.* to name, 609.

noblésse, *sb.* magnificence, 782.

nobléye, *sb.* noble condition, 828.

nolde (= *ne wolde*), would not, 83.

nones, nonce, in *for the nones,* earlier *for then ones,* for that once, for the occasion [5].

norice, *sb.* nurse, 561.

norisse, *v.* to nurture, bring up, 399; cp. *fed* 397.

nowche, *sb.* jewelled clasp, buckle, 382.

nyl = *ne wyl,* will not, 119, 363.

nys = *ne is,* is not, 448.

o, *see* on.

óbeisánce, *sb.* obedience; submission, 24; act of obedience, 230.

óbeisànt, *adj.* obedient, 66.

office, *sb.* service : *houses of office,* domestic offices, 264 n.

of-newe, *adv.* lately, 938 n.

oghte, *pret.* (it) was due, 1120 n.; it behoves, 1150.

on, oon, o, *adj.* and *pron.* one, 87, 569; *many oon* many a one, 775. *See* 602 n., 212 n.; *and* at-on. **ones,**

gen. once ; *at ones* together, 1178. *See* nones.

on-lofte, *adv.* up ; *kepe on-lofte,* to sustain, 229.

ordinaunce, *sb.* (good) order, 961.

outrely, *adv.* utterly, to the full, 639 ; absolutely, 953 ; inordinately, 335 ; emphatically, 768.

outreye, *v.* to go beyond bounds ; *out of youreself outreye* to be beside yourself, to behave like one distracted, 643.

outward, *adv.* abroad, 424.

overal, *adv.* in all circumstances, 1048.

overeste, *adj. superl.* topmost, *Prol.* 290*.

pace *v.* (= *passe*), to depart (from this life), 1092.

par áventùre, *see* áventùre.

passynge, *pres. p.* surpassing, 240, 1225.

penýble, *adj.* painstaking, anxious to please, 714.

peyne, *v. reflex.* to take pains, 976.

pistel, *sb.* epistle, 1154.

pitous, *adj.* sad, 97 ; touching, 1086 ; tender, 1080.

plesa(u)nce, *sb.* pleasure, 658.

pley, *sb.* game, 10 ; rules of the game, 11 ; sport, jest, 1030.

pleyn, *adj.* full, complete, 926. [Lat. *plenus.*]

pleyn, *adj.* plain : *in short and pleyn,* 577. [Lat. *planus.*]

pleyne, *v.* to complain, 97 n.

plye, *v.* to bend, 1169.

povre-fostred, *adj.* nurtured in poverty, 1043.

povreliche, *adv.* poorly, 213.

pr(e)eve, *v.* to prove, 28 ; to stand testing, 1000.

preeve, *sb.* proof, 787.

presente (*with*), *v.* to bring into the presence of, deliver to, 578.

pridelees, *adj.* without undue pride, 930.

pris, *sb.* praise, 1026 n.

privee, *adj.* confidential, 192.

privetee, *sb.* privacy. 249.

prohemye, *sb.* proem, preface, 43.

prosperitee, *sb.* happiness, 1034.

purpos, *sb.* resolution, 1078 ; *to that purpos* to that effect, 573.

quod, *pa. t. 3 sg.* said, 22.

rather, *adv.* sooner, 1169.

recchelees, *adj.* (reckless), careless, negligent, 488. *See* rekke(n).

rede, *v.* to advise, 811.

redresse, *v.* restore, improve, 431.

reed, *sb.* advice, 653.

rekke(n), *v.* to care. *See* roghte.

reste, *sb.* peace, 112 ; peace of mind, happiness, 160, 434.

rethorike, *sb.* eloquence, 32.

reule, *v.* to rule ; *reule hire,* to order her life, 327.

reuthe, *see* routhe.

reverence, *sb.* honour, 196, 231.

rewen, *v.* to take pity, 1050.

right, *adj.* direct, 273.

roghte, *pa. t.* (of *rekke*), *impers. with dat.* it recks, it matters to, 685. *See* 105 n.

roialtee, *sb.* magnificence, 928.

rome, *v.* to walk, 118.

root, *sb.* foot (of a mountain), 58 n.

routhe, reuthe, *sb.* pity, compassion, 579 n., 893 ; pitiful sight, 562.

rude, *adj.* uncultured, unintelligent, 750 ; coarse, of poor quality, 916.

rudenesse, *sb.* rusticity, 397.

rumbul, *sb.* rumour, 997.

ryve, *v.* to cleave, 1236.

sad, *adj.* firm, steadfast, 220 ; unchanging, 602 ; unmoved, 693 ; serious, 237, 293.

sadly, *adv.* firmly, tightly, 1100.

sadnesse, *sb.* constancy, 452.

sad-stidefast, *adj.* firm (of mind), 564

saufly, *adv.* (safely), without fear of contradiction, 870.

sautrie, *sb.* a psaltery ; a kind of harp, fitted with a sounding board behind the strings, *Prol.* 296*.

say, saugh, *pa. t. sg.* saw, 667, 1033.

scathe, *sb.* (harm), a pity; *it is scathe* = French *c'est dommage*, 1172.

sclaundre, *sb.* evil report, 722, 730.

scoléye, *v.* to study (at a school or university), *Prol.* 302*.

secreely, *adv.* secretly, 763.

secte, *sb.* sex, 1171.

seelde (*tyme*), *adv.* seldom, 146, 427.

seeth, *pa. t. sg.* boiled, 227.

sely, *adj.* innocent, 948.

semblánt, *sb.* outward show, 928.

sentence, *sb.* meaning, *Prol.* 306*; feeling, 636; *this sentence* words to this effect, 791.

sergeant, *sb.* attendant, 519.

servàge, *sb.* service, 482.

servitute, *sb.* obligation to serve, 798.

servysable, *adj.* active in service, 979.

sharply, *adv.* peremptorily, 1192.

shewe, *v.* to declare, set forth, explain, 90, 104, 591.

shilde, *v.* to forfend, forbid, prevent, 839, 1232*.

shoope, *pa. t.* (of *shape*) created, 903; arranged, 198, 946; *pp.* shapen, 275.

shredde, *pa. t.* prepared for cooking by peeling *or* by slicing small, 227.

shrewe, *sb.* a virago, 1222*.

shul, *pret. pres. pl.* shall, 38, 125.

sikerly, *adv.* certainly, 184.

sikly, *adv.* ill; *sikly berth*, 625 n.

sit, *3 sg. pres. indic.* (it) befits, 460 n.

sith, *conj.* since, 171, 349, 626, &c.

sithe, *sb.* time; *ofte sithe* often, 233.

skile, *sb.* reason, 1152 n.

sklendre, *adj.* weak, of little force, 1198.

slake, *v.* cease; die out, 137; desist (from), 705; *trans.* to put an end to, 802, 1107.

slee(n), *v.* to smite, 628; to slay: *pp.* slawen, 544; slayn, 536.

sleighte, *sb.* (exercise of) skill, 1102.

smal, *adj.* slim, 380; small, 382.

smerte, *adv.* sharply, so as to cause pain, 629.

smok, *sb.* smock, shift, chemise, 886.

smoklees, *adj.* without a smock, 875.

so, *adv.* introducing a wish, 30, 843. See 7 n.

solempne, *adj.* magnificent, 1125.

somdeel, *adv.* somewhat, much, 1012.

soory, *adj.* sorry, sore, 1244; [from *soore* 'sore'; not connected with *sorrow*.]

soothly, *adv.* for a truth, 689.

sophýme, *sb.* philosophical problem, 5.

sovereyn, *adj.* supreme, surpassing, 112.

sownynge (*in*), *pres. p.* tending towards, *Prol.* 307*.

space, *sb.* space of time, 103, 918.

spille, *v.* to destroy, 503.

stable, *adj.* constant in love, 931.

stalke, *v.* to step stealthily, 525 n.

stente, *see* stynte.

stille, *adj.* quiet, silent, 2, 121 n.; undisturbed, 891; *lat it be stille* leave it be, let it alone, 891, [7]. *adv.* in silence, silently, 293, 525; secretly, 1077; still, always, 580.

stoor, *sb.* store, reserve, 17.

stounde, *sb.* moment, 1098.

straunge, *adj.* of alien blood, 138.

streen, *sb.* stock, strain, 157.

stre(e)pe, *v.* to strip, 863, 1116.

streyne, *v.* to constrain, 144.

studie(n), *v.* to think deeply, ponder, 5, 8.

sturdinesse, *sb.* harshness, 700.

sturdy, *adj.* stern, 1049.

stynte, stente (*of*), *v.* cease, desist from, 703, 734, 747 [*stente* is Kentish].

subgetz, *sb. pl.* subjects, 482.

subtil, *adj.* secret, 737.   [691.

subtiltee, *sb.* hidden purpose, deceit,

súffisance, *sb.* contentment, 759 n.

súffisaunt, *adj.* capable (of), 960.

suffraunce, *sb.* patience under trials, 1162.

suspect, *sb.* suspicion, 905 n.

swappe, *v.* to strike, cut (the head off), 586; swapte, *pa. t.* fell heavily, 1099.

swelwe, *v.* to swallow, 1188.

swough, *sb.* swoon, 1100.

swownynge, *sb.* swoon, 1080.
syke, *v.* to sigh (in grief), 545.
syn, *conj.* since, 1196.

tempte, *v.* to test, 452 n., 458.
tendre, *adj.* over-fastidious, 927 n. ; young, 989.
tentifly, *adv.* attentive, 334.
termes, *sb. pl.* technical expressions (usually those of philosophy), 16.
thanne, *adv.* then, 127.
thee, *v.* to thryve, 1226*.
ther, *adv.* and *conj.*, where ; *ther as* where, 173, 198.
therwith, *adv.* besides, 71.
thewes, *sb. pl.* moral qualities, 409.
thilke, *adj. demonstr.* that (same), 197.
tho, *adv.* then, 544, 764.
thresshfold, *sb.* threshold, 288.
throope, *sb.* (thorp), village, 199, 208.
throwe, *sb.* a (little) while, 450.
thurgh, *prep.* through, 69.
thynke, *v.* to purpose, intend ; **thoughte,** *pa. t. sg.* 144, 455.
thynke, *pa. t.* **thoughte,** *v. impers. with dat.* it seems, 54, 353, 406, 908. *See* 105 n.
tonne, *sb.* (ale- *or* wine-) cask, 215 n.
to-race, *v.* to tear to pieces, 572.
toward, *prep.* in preparation for, 778.
translated, *pp.* transmuted, 385.
traváille, *sb.* labour, 1210 ; cp. 195 n.
tree, *sb.* : *of tree* wooden, 558.
tretys, *sb.* (marriage) treaties *or* agreements, 331.
trouble, *adj.* troubled, 465.
turne, *v.* : *turne agayn* return, 872.
tweye, *numeral adj.* two, 982.

ugly, *adj.* causing terror, fearsome, 673.
undern, *sb.* mid-morning ; about 9 a m., 260 n., 981.
undigne, *adj.* undeserving, 359.
undiscreet, *adj.* lacking in discernment *or* judgement, 996.
unnethe(s), *adv.* with difficulty, hardly, 318, 384, 892, 1106.
unsad, *adj.* inconstant, 995.
untressed, *pp adj.* unplaited, 379.

vane, *sb.* wind-vane, 996.
verray, *adj.* true, 343.
vitáille, *sb.* (victuals), food, 59, 265.
vouche-sauf, *v.* to allow, 306 ; deign, 885.
voyden, *v.* get rid of, 910 ; vacate, 806.

waite, *v.* to watch, 708 n.
wax, *see* wexen.
weede, *sb.* clothes, 863.
weepe, *strong pa. t.* wept, 545.
wel, *adv.* (with intensive force), 892, &c.
wele, *sb.* weal, happiness, 842.
welkne, *sb.* (*dative*), sky, 1124.
welle, *sb.* spring, 48, 215.
wende, *v.* to go, 1027.
wene, *v.* to think, 1174 ; **wende,** *pa. t.* 544, 751, 1094 ; *pp.* 691.
werk, *sb.* deed(s), 28, 107.
werk, *v.* to act, do, 504.
werkyng, *sb.* action(s), practice, 495.
wexen, *v.* to wax, increase, 998 ; **wax,** *pa. t. sg.* became, 317 ; **woxen,** *pp.* 400.
what, *indef. adj.* whatsoever, 10, 165 ; *interrog. adv.* why, 383, 1221*.
whenne, *adv.* whence, 588 n.
where as, *conj.* where, 48, 829 n. [846.
whilom, *adv.* in former times, once, 64,
wight, *sb.* a person *or* thing, 240, &c. ; *no wight,* nobody, 177, 769, &c.
wikke, *adj. earlier form of* wicked, 785.
willynge, *sb.* will, wish, 319.
wiste, *see* woot.
wit, *sb.* wisdom, 149, 428.
wityng, *sb.* knowledge, 492.
wo, *adj.* woful, 753.
wol(e) ; wolt, *2 sg.* ; *pres. sg. & pl.* will, 24, 129.
woned, *pp.* accustomed, 339.
woot, *pret. pres.* know(s), 155, 862 ; **wost,** *2 sg.* in *wostow* ? = *wost thou* ? knowest thou? ; **wiste,** *pa. t.* 814, [6].
worshipe, *v.* to honour, 166.
worshipful, *adj.* worthy to be honoured, 401.
wortes, *sb. pl.* roots, 226.
wostow, *see* woot.
woxon, *see* wexen.

wrye, *v.* to cover, 887.

wrynge, *v.* to wring the hands, 1212.

wyfhod, *sb.* wifehood, 699.

wyl, *sb.* willingness, 176; wish, resolution, 509.

wysly, *adv.* certainly, 822.

y-, prefix of the past participle, as in: y-born, born, 72; y-dressed, set, arranged, 381; y-feyned, evaded (by deceit), 529; y-fostred, nurtured, 213; y-go, (gone), devoted, *Prol.* 286*; y-ronne, run (through), pierced, 214; y-set, established, 409.

yaf, *see* yeve.

yate, *sb.* gate, 1013.

yelden, *v.* to yield (up), 843.

yerd(e), *sb.* rod; *hence* authority, 22 n.

yeve, *v.* to give, 30; yaf, *pa. t.* 203; yeven, *pp.* 758.

y-feere, *adv.* together, 1113.

y-like, *adv.* equally, unchangingly, 602.

ymaginyng, *pres. p.* pondering, wondering, 598.

ynogh, *adv.* enough, 75.

yond, *adv.* far away, 1199 n.

yoore, *adv.* for a long time, 68; long ago, 1140.

Petrarch (left) and Boccaccio at work.
From a miniature in Brit. Mus. MS. Add. 35321.